Though many space beings, who are only souls like us that inhabit thought-worlds, actually incarnate here in the normal fashion, some walk into full-grown bodies, others are beamed down from spaceships, which are only thought-ships that materialize as they enter into this dimension, and still others come here by mental projection. The highest are the ascended Masters who are free from all limitation and can be anywhere they like in an instant. These Great Ones merge into omnipresence and emerge wherever they like through the simplest technique of identification.

Anyone who can grasp what is about to be discussed is getting a glimpse into his own future. . . .

ALIENS AMONG US

ALIENS AMONG US

Ruth Montgomery

FAWCETT CREST • NEW YORK

A Fawcett Crest Book
Published by Ballantine Books
Copyright © 1985 by Ruth Montgomery

Library of Congress Catalog Card Number: 84-26565

ISBN 0-449-20809-5

This edition published by arrangement with G.P. Putnam's Sons

Manufactured in the United States of America

First Ballantine Books Edition: August 1986

Contents

Foreword

THIS is a book about extraterrestrials: who they are, where they come from, how they arrive, and why they are here. Midway in this next-to-last decade before the end of the twentieth century, and the long-predicted shift of the earth on its axis, extraterrestrial communication seems to be a world-wide phenomenon. Unlike our government, I do not feel that the subject can be longer ignored. Pulling the bedcovers over our heads does not rid us of the presence of space aliens, nor should we want to turn them away. They are said to be here to help us earthlings, and in my opinion we need all the help we can get in our strife-ridden, pol-luted, self-centered society.

We are all one! My Guides repeatedly stress that our space brothers and sisters share with us a mutual Creator, and that far from being a unique form of life in an otherwise uninhabited cosmos, we humans are comparatively backward souls who came to Schoolhouse Earth to learn much needed lessons.

The more enlightened ones among us, according to the Guides, have had numerous lives on other planets as well as earth, and have returned here to rescue us from our limited thought patterns before it is too late. Some of our "unearthly" visitors, they say, have emerged from spaceships to test our environment, take samplings of our flora and fauna to reseed in other galaxies, and conduct harmless experiments with human beings, manifesting themselves and their spacecraft here by reassembling the pattern of the atoms. But a significantly larger group of spacelings, the Guides insist, volunteered to be born into earthly bodies, or to become Walk-ins through the utilization of unwanted human forms. In other words, they are like us, and during the past year or so I have been swamped by letters and calls from men and women who sincerely believe that their "real home" is in another planetary system.

For those who are unfamiliar with my previous books in the psychic field, I should explain that the ones I call "my Guides" are souls like ourselves who have had many previous lifetimes but are currently in the spirit plane, as we will be when we pass through the mysterious door called death. They introduced themselves to me a quarter-century ago, after famed medium Arthur Ford said that I had the ability to do "automatic writing" and told me how to go about it. Since then the Guides are always on tap for the daily sessions, and after

Ford's death in January 1971 he also joined the group.

In succeeding years, utilizing the voluminous material that the Guides write through my typing fingers, we have jointly produced eight books on subjects of their own choosing that run the gamut from life after death to reincarnation, and from a prehistoric view of the world to Walk-ins who rejuvenate dying or unwanted bodies in order to help humankind. A political rival once said of my friend Barry Goldwater that he was "dragged kicking and screaming into the eighteenth century." My Guides might say the same about my own resistance each time that they have urged me to break new ground by writing about psychic concepts that seem to be ahead of their times. After all, as a long-time syndicated Washington columnist on politics and world affairs I had a reputation to maintain, and no desire to be regarded as a kook.

But somehow the Guides have always been vindicated in their judgment. When I reluctantly wrote *A Search for the Truth* in 1965 I feared ostracism by the religious community. Instead, I was flooded by invitations from protestant ministers to speak from their pulpits, and from Catholic academia to address their student bodies. After I published *Here and Hereafter*, a big best-seller in the field of reincarnation, bookstalls began to burgeon with volumes on that formerly controversial subject. And when *A World Beyond*, my book describing what happens immediately after death, also became a best-seller, suddenly doctors and psychiatrists rushed into print with books about the experiences of their patients who came back from clinical death to describe what they had experienced.

The role of Pathfinder can be a lonely one, but

each time my faithful Guides have pushed me only one step forward at a time. They did not inundate me with vast quantities of material on a wide range of subjects, but simply nudged me along, allowing me to complete a book on one subject before challenging me with another. Yet each broke new ground. The term "Walk-in" had never seen the light of print until my Guides and I introduced the concept in *Strangers Among Us*, and followed that with specific cases delineated in *Threshold to Tomorrow*. I feared a hooting reaction from the nonbelievers, but nowadays it is virtually impossible to pick up any publication in the parapsychology field without running across references to Walk-ins, and a number of distinguished psychiatrists and psychologists are exploring the phenomenon as an explanation for their patients' radically altered personalities and goals after a near brush with death.

All of this is by way of saying that I hope the subject of extraterrestrials will meet with the same open-mindedness. It was a difficult barrier for me to cross. When the Guides first began dictating material on the subject, I said "a thousand times no" and turned away from our daily sessions. Then the same phenomenon occurred that has baffled me throughout my long association with my spirit pen pals. Thousands of letters began to pour in from unknown readers, begging me to write a book about extraterrestrials, and hundreds of these readers professed to be space people who insisted that the time was right for a comprehensive book on the subject. When I accused my Guides of masterminding the write-in campaign, they figuratively shrugged and admitted it. But how did it happen? And why?

I seemed to be the least qualified person extant to write on such an all-embracing subject. I had never seen a UFO. I had no "proof" that I had ever spoken with a space alien, although some I had spoken with claimed to be. I had never had an out-of-body experience in which I seemingly visited other planets. I entertained no hazy "memory" of having been inside a spaceship. I had experienced no "loss of time" while on a lonely road where UFO sightings had been reported. Why me?

The pressure mounted. Many of the letter writers pleaded with me to ask the Guides why their lives had so drastically altered since an encounter with a UFO. Laura, the wise young Walk-in about whom I wrote at length in *Strangers Among Us,* insisted that I owed it to my readers at least to tell them what the Guides were saying about extraterrestrials, "because they are real." Joyce Updike wrote beseeching letters asking me to put the subject into proper perspective, "because people trust your Guides." Respected magazines and newspapers blossomed forth with a rash of scientific articles about the probability of life on other planets, containing such quotes as these: "Many scientists now believe that extraterrestrial life exists, perhaps hundreds or even thousands of civilizations" (Bernard Oliver of Hewlett-Packard, who works with NASA); "The time will have to come when we realize that we're not the center of the universe. The galaxy may be teeming with life. There may be millions of civilizations" (Astronomer Richard Terrile of the Jet Propulsion Laboratory); and "A suitable habitat for life and a mechanism for its origin may exist near many of the billions of stars in our galaxy" (Paul Horowitz, professor of physics at Harvard

University, a recognized leader in the search for extraterrestrial intelligence).

While I continued to drag my feet, curious things began to happen. Having completed research on my Shick family genealogy, I staged a family reunion that was attended by more than sixty far-flung cousins representing four generations, many of whom had never met before. Some brought cameras, and later sent me snapshots of the various events, but one of them was eye-boggling. Snapped by my second cousin Frank Wagner, Jr., of Phoenix, whom I had not previously known, it clearly depicts me standing at the head table addressing the relatives about our mutual ancestors, while towering above me is a sharply defined white-robed figure. At the right of the picture, other ethereal figures seem to be gathered in a listening huddle. Frank enclosed the two snapshots taken immediately before and after that picture, to demonstrate that there was no distortion of the lens, and he gave technical reasons why the forms could not be an accumulation of smoke from cigarettes. Could the figures indeed have been shadowy materializations of our pleased progenitors, as my Guides insist?

The next odd incident occurred on a rainy February day in 1984 when, against my inclination, I went to New York to make a series of radio recordings in connection with the new paperback edition of my previous book. I intended to fly up and back on the hourly shuttle, and the Guides told me not to worry about it, "because we'll get you back safe and sound the same day." After leaving the recording studio I noticed such darkening clouds that I decided to forego dinner with my editor and return immediately to LaGuardia airport, to catch the four o'clock shuttle. On reaching there, I learned that because of dense fog no planes had been able to land for several hours, and as a consequence there was none available for departure. Hundreds of people stood willy-nilly in the shuttle lines, but gradually as hope faded many of them left the airport. No Planes Landing repeatedly flickered on the arrival and departure boards. What to do?

Suddenly remembering my spirit pals, whom I have a habit of forgetting, I sent out a telepathic message: "All right, you Guides. You promised to get me safely home today if I agreed to make this promotional trip for our book. How about it?" Within two minutes, a voice on the loudspeaker announced: "A plane is making its landing approach. Be prepared to board immediately before the fog closes in again." We gratefully trooped aboard and made a safe touchdown in Washington within forty minutes. Later I checked with the airport and learned that ours was the only New York shuttle plane that had flown to Washington that entire afternoon or evening. The next day the Guides wrote: "We'd promised you a day without problems, and we kept watch. When that circling plane was about to bypass New York we opened a space [in the fog] for it to come through."

One other incident perhaps bears repeating. My little dog, Muffy, died of a heart attack in April, and I was devastated. In fact, I could scarcely bear to glance into the sunroom, which had been his favorite place to lie, with his back to the plants and his eyes invariably focused on my chair in the adjoining library. I had never paid any attention to our seven large plants, which my husband, Bob, watered and fed, but a few days after Muffy's demise I did notice that they were withered and yellowing. Realizing that I had an abundance of love that I could no longer lavish on Muffy, I told the plants that they would henceforth be my pets. "I love you very much," I fibbed, "and from now on I am going to give you tender loving care." I was carefully removing their dead leaves when Bob came in and said not to bother. "They're practically dead," he declared. "I'm going to toss them out today and get some others."

I asked if he would mind delaying while I tried a little experiment, and within a few days the plants began to show exuberant life, putting out new shoots at a phenomenal rate. I did not alter Bob's established method of watering and fertilizing them, but I talked to them several times a day, telling them how beautiful they were and how proud we were of them. Today they are strong, healthy, growing plants with shiny dark green leaves.

The purpose of recalling these little vignettes, which concern my personal evolvement, is to demonstrate that gradually, under the influence of my Guides, I have come to believe firmly in unseen forces that are not apparent to the human eye. During these years my unseen friends have gradually convinced me of the reality of communication between the living and the so-called dead, as well as between plants and humans. I have become a firm believer in reincarnation, and in the concept that a high-minded soul in the spirit realm can exchange places with another soul who wishes to depart the physical plane, by entering as a Walk-in. Why should I then maintain a closed mind to the possibility that space friends from other planets and galaxies are visiting earth to help us solve our problems? Just because I personally had not encountered a UFO did not mean that the reports of

others whom I respected could not be as reliable as
my own would have been.

The Guides long ago told me that we human
souls all began simultaneously as "sparks from
God." Now they were writing: "The souls in other
galaxies are just as much a part of the Creator as
are we. They originated as we did in that original
burst of creative energy in which all souls began as
companions and co-creators with God. When some
of them felt attracted to certain planets and galaxies they went there as pioneers, to help subdue and
regulate the elements and the beasts of the field,
and because there proved to be great sympathy
between themselves and the sometimes difficult
terrain and atmospheric conditions they remained
for longer and longer periods, to turn those stumbling blocks into stepping stones. It was somewhat
different with our own planet earth, which came
later into being. Here souls first entered the bodies
of animals and birds and fishes, as we told you in
The World Before, and because of this tampering
with God's act of creation earthlings fell from grace
for a long period of time, until a prototype was
created as Adam, with Eve as his mate. These are
simply names for the first man and woman to inhabit what we term a human body, and those who
visit here from other planets are able to create a
duplicate of this body that is so well suited to
earth's atmosphere and the need for walking about.
Thus, although body types differ on other planets,
this is found to be the most satisfactory one for
earth, and in the early days these bodies were kept
healthy and functioning for many hundreds of years;
whereas now the pollution, the rampant diseases
brought on by man's infidelity to his Creator, and

other man-created hazards render them less fit for lengthy survival.''

On another day the Guides wrote: "The so-called space people are in actuality ones like yourselves, who are also space people in the sense that all of us inhabit a universe that is whirling in orbit. When these souls who inhabit other spheres visit the earth they come as humanoids, because otherwise they would be captured or repelled or humiliated by those who would make of them a laughing stock. To understand why they arrive on earth is to explore the plan of universal brotherhood, since all of us began as sparks cast off by the Creator. As these souls acquired identity and free will they moved from one space to another, and some of them shone brilliantly as true companions of the Creator, while others developed delusions of grandeur as co-creators and sought to impose their own will on others. Some visited the earth, while others sought experience on different planets and orbs. They are no more alien than you or we are, except that the earth is not their original planet.

"Not all space travelers are from any one planet. They come as explorers and observers and intend no harm, although harm sometimes results, inadvertently. They are not of this galaxy, as there is no humanoid type of life on the planets in the same galaxy as earth, although there once was. Those who visit earth at this time are from planets with highly advanced technology and science. They have solved the challenge of space travel through dissolving atoms and reconstituting them in the earth's atmosphere, and on other planets. They are willing to share their knowledge with earth scientists if given half a chance, but are not willing to risk destruction of their craft and their lives to make approaches where they could be shot down. That is why you are hearing less now than formerly of UFO sightings."

I asked for further details about their method of travel, and the Guides wrote: "Space aliens are able to dissolve the atomic structures of their spaceships as well as their bodies and to reassemble the atoms as they reach earth's outer stratosphere. It is a feat that some earthlings with extraordinary psychic talents have also been able to perform within earth's atmosphere. We speak now of the avatars and certain Hindu Yogis in particular. Usually such enlightened ones have recalled the memory of how to perform that feat [of appearing and disappearing] from previous lifetimes on other planets that are more advanced scientifically as well as spiritually than earth. Bear in mind that the two are not necessarily synonymous. To be technically advanced is not necessarily spiritually advanced. As an example, study the differences between ancient Lemuria with its spiritual leadership and Atlantis in its latter days, when its technology was further advanced than anywhere before or since in the earth plane; yet it had lost its spiritual leadership and was beset with greed and personal ambition. Some galaxies can similarly be contrasted. On some planets the inhabitants are so close to the Creator that they commune easily with His spirit plane, while on others they are so far advanced technologically that they can dissolve atoms, relocate them by mental powers alone, and reassemble them wherever they wish, yet have lost the ability to commune directly with the Godhead. Then there are planets which combine the best qualities of both, and a few that unfortunately combine the worst of both worlds. Not all of those now coming to earth are of the highest spiritual quality. Some are here to instill awareness and love of the Creator, while others are here to advance us in the earth realm technologically and stop our pollution. Some are on purely exploratory missions to sample our atmosphere and observe preparations for the earth's shift. They are harbingers of a new order, and their services will be welcomed in putting earth back into operation after the shift, but those whose spiritual advancement is beyond and above that of present earthlings will have the major role in establishing the New Age and the New Order in the earth.''

The Guides said that most of the space travelers now visiting earth are from "places in the spectrum of galaxies beyond the Milky Way. They are from far older civilizations than the earth's and often live thousands of years, since there are no killer germs in the galaxies from which they hail. These germs are not permitted to flourish there because thought forms eradicated them as they appeared. Although germs are living organisms they are thought into being by low forms of energy and should not be permitted to exist, since they were not of God's original making, but were brought into being by man's lower nature. In the galaxies of which we speak the souls have kept themselves on far higher planes than has humankind, although we stress that earth is by no means the lowest form of creation, nor inhabited by the least developed creatures. Many planets are at lower stages of development than earth, as are their inhabitants, but they are obviously not yet able to communicate with earth; and that is fortunate, because earth is not yet sufficiently developed to lend them a helping hand in the upward climb. Those who are ap-

pearing in human form on earth at this time are
from highly evolved planets. They seek to further
their soul progression, and will in time play a large
part in the development of humankind."

The Guides say that although space beings have
visited earth for millennia, they are now "rushing
in as seldom before to awaken earthlings and help
them to realize that their destruction is imminent"
unless better ways are developed to settle disputes
between peoples. "They are aghast at the direction
that planet earth and its people have taken in the
last few decades," the Guides continued, "including nuclear weapons threats against other nations
and curtailment of human freedom. They will not
be able to prevent the shift of the earth, as that is
due to natural causes along with man's depletion of
water, oil and other resources beneath the earth's
crust, but they will try to prevent the warlike
skirmishes from developing into World War III."

I asked about the different means utilized by
space beings to enter our culture, and the Guides
said that some are being born into human bodies
for the first time, some had lived here upon occasion before, some are arriving as Walk-ins, and
others are temporarily exchanging bodies with earthlings "with or without permission." Surprised at
the latter phrase, I asked for elucidation, and they
explained that these transfers occur "during a brief
coma when a human of appropriate talents is within
range of the equipment on spaceships." Explaining
why so many humans have "memories" of being
aboard spaceships, or have undergone a strange
"loss of time" after glimpsing a UFO, the Guides
declared: "They regard it later as a brief amnesia,
but actually they are experiencing at another level
of consciousness. While they are within the space-

ship, the so-called space alien is able to utilize the earthly body for experimentation and to understand its mechanism, so that when the time is right other extraterrestrials will be able to come en masse to replace earthlings who want to escape the shift of the earth on its axis. Lured to areas adjoining their hidden spacecraft, the bodies of these earthlings are temporarily assumed while their minds or spirits are assisted aboard the ships and given intense questioning. The bodies are also examined, but often while occupied by a spaceling so that no pain is felt.''

I asked if this meant that the humans were physically, or merely mentally taken aboard UFOs, and they replied that both methods have been employed.

From time to time the Guides introduce a space alien who, they say, is cooperating with them in bringing me the information for this book. ''He is planning on visiting the earth plane shortly, when he finds the right person to exchange places with him,'' they wrote one day. ''He will be an observer of the coming shift and is anxious to be in the flesh there at that time, to do what he can to direct fleeing earthlings to safe areas and help them establish themselves in new colonies. His own planet is full of colonies of humanoids living peaceably together, and he feels that he is the right soul to teach cooperative skills and peaceable ways, without looting and stealing. On his own planet there is no such thing as robbing others, for each realizes that he is a part of the whole and that to steal from another only diminishes oneself. The people live in communities that are something like beehives in that they are densely packed with boxlike dwellings, protected from the elements, and rich in natural resources that thrive in the half-light and climate

control below the surface of their planet. They are
good and helpful people who have much to teach
earth people. Some of them are already where you
are and will direct operations as the time nears for
the shift of the earth on its axis. They feel an
affinity for your planet because some of them originally came there in eons past and helped to colo-
nize it. They worship the one God and are of a
much older civilization than that of earth. Earth is
a late comer to habitation and sets a foul example
for others with its squabbling, war making, selfishness and greed. Some earthlings are working their
way out of the cycles of rebirth by goodness and
helpfulness, and will be permitted to join other
planetary galaxies if they wish, but certain ones
are too craven to be wished on other planets that
are more advanced.''

A space being called Rolf who occasionally writes
to me through the Guides declared: "Ruth, it is
vital that you get the message across to others that
we are coming in great numbers, not with any
intention of harm, but to help rescue earth from
pollution and nuclear explosions. We want all to
live in harmony. The earth is one of the best proving grounds for this because it has nearly everything needed to produce harmony, if only those
souls in training there would develop their senses
and promote ideas for peace. We of other galaxies
are fearful that the earth will become so polluted
by nuclear armaments that it will affect the stratosphere and endanger other forms of celestial life.
We want to turn earth's peoples toward love for
each other, and will do all that we are able to effect
this.''

The Guides say that all earthlings either already
have experienced, or eventually will experience

life in other planetary systems. Sometimes this is only in spirit form between lives, as described in *The World Before*, "but there are also earthlings being born into other planetary systems. They have earned that right through their own soul development and are finding the glorious love and helpfulness that is so often lacking on the earth. But they are temporary tenants in the other galaxies, for earthlings usually remain as such and will eventually complete their cycle of rebirths on their own earth after broadening their experience on other planets."

They then surprised me by claiming that I have lived on other planets. When I remonstrated that I have no such recollections, they wrote: "You are unable to recall your past lives in other galaxies because you have not truly awakened to the role that you are portraying. Do you believe that we could so easily have worked through you unless you had been other than an earthling at some time in the past? We too have inhabited other galaxies and we therefore penetrate the earth's atmosphere more easily than those in spirit who are strictly earthlings. There is a reason why we told you years ago that you had been on Atlantis but not on Lemuria, for at that time you were residing in another galaxy, and when you saw the destructive elements being introduced into the culture of Atlantis, the soul who is you voluntarily became an earthling in order to help prevent the destruction of the advanced culture that the earth enjoyed prior to the shift of the earth that destroyed Lemuria and endangered Atlantis. You had lived in the Orion constellation then, and you were on Sirius immediately prior to your present lifetime. Orion is a fascinating cluster of planets in that the beings there are ethereal and do not know sex as such.

They are all of one kind and reproduce themselves through spiritual matings that produce gossamerlike tendrils developing into etheric bodies. They are deeply concerned with the Creator's will, and manifest on earth as spiritual thought forms. These they can transform into physical bodies, since 'thoughts are things,' and instantly travel through space. Sirius is quite different, in that those inhabiting it are seldom permanent residents. It is a meeting place for those who have mastered their own planetary systems and are preparing there for whatever further duties they care to assume. Many return to their home planets to assist those still struggling there, since we are all one, and others elect to progress to other realms and galaxies. Sirius is one of the more important way stations for earthlings who wish to continue their spiritual development and not just to rest and relax in the spirit plane. It is a working realm that prepares those who would contribute to the fulfillment of the soul and help others to do likewise. It has some atmosphere and is not too unlike earth in that respect."

Well, honestly! Gossamerlike tendrils! Before I had a chance to tell the Guides that if they have heads they should be examined, a further shocker was introduced. "We are with a so-called space alien now who is considering going into the earth strata," they wrote. "His normal habitat when in physical being has been beyond the Andromeda galaxy, and he wishes to say that those in being there assume a shape not too different from that on earth, but with greatly enlarged diaphragms and lungs because the oxygen is so weak that an earthling could not exist there in his own body for any length of time. It is a planet called Alabram and is peopled by millions of beings who are souls like ourselves, except that in the beginning they went to that planet while earth was still in molten form. There is a tendency to return again and again to the same planet where one is familiar with the surroundings and the kindred souls. Their birthing is somewhat different than that of humans, as they carry the fetus for a shorter gestation period in their stomachs and regurgitate it when the time is served. At that moment it is extremely small, but it grows rapidly and reaches maturity at what by earth time would be only seven years. These beings have large brains for their size and absorb information through osmosis, reading the advanced minds of others and holding an awareness of this learning from one lifetime to another. They drink liquid similar to water and thrive on foods that are grown in caves and tunnels hollowed out beneath the planet's crust, because the star that serves as their sun would burn the tender plants to a crisp if they were planted above ground.''

I somewhat sarcastically observed that next they would be telling me that UFOs have bases beneath our oceans, as some psychics have alleged, and they replied: ''The extraterrestrials do not have a base in your oceans, and we have previously told you that there is nothing to the hollow-earth theory, of a civilization operating beneath the surface of the earth. The extraterrestrials come and go at will because of their ability to disintegrate solids and reassemble them wherever they wish. This is a law of the universe that is not yet fully understood in planet earth, but it does not defy natural laws. They travel from other planetary systems to the earth plane by thought, just as your thoughts can put you in Hong Kong, Russia, South America or other places where you have memories of previous visits. But unlike you, they can "think" the apparatus that they have previously dissolved into being in the earth's atmosphere, and this ability will one day be understood and used by earthlings in the New Age to come. Thought transference is no more a miraculous event than loving another at a distance, or of feeling oneself bathed in that absent person's love. When an earthling advances to the spirit state it is not strange to recreate memories into actual things, or physical embodiments. Similarly, extraterrestrials from more advanced realms are constantly visiting earth, and can go and come at will due to their understanding of the Law of Thought."

Having interviewed a number of otherwise normal people who seemingly recall visits aboard spacecraft and are able to describe the ships and their occupants in detail, I asked the Guides to explain how this can occur. Ever patient, they began: "We will start by reviewing what has been said earlier about those who for a time exchange places with earthlings. A human who temporarily surrenders his or her body either sleeps, or explores space machines, or takes trips on UFOs that can be recalled as in a dream, or under hypnosis, upon resuming the function of the body. The time to them seems very long, whereas it may be only a few minutes or hours, but during that space of time the visiting alien has satisfied himself or herself as to how to manipulate an earth body, investigated how it is put together and what stimuli to use in commanding it to do various chores. To the alien it is a fascinating experience, just as it would be for an earthling to step down on some remote planet full of smoky substances called people and try operating that filmy body for a time. These visiting aliens are here for a purpose: to protect earth from itself. Not all are highly motivated, you understand, for there are all kinds of souls in various stages of development on other planets as well as earth; but most of those who visit earth at this period are here for scientific purposes, to probe the earth's atmospheric conditions and examine the potential for turning it into a landing place for outer space people to visit and explore. However, they are well aware that time is running out, and that if visits are to be made before the shift there is work to be done in readying the earth people as well as the continents for such visits. After the shift they are planning to return to unpopulated new lands that will rise from the oceans and be yet unclaimed, to set up their own laboratories and think tanks. But for now they wish only to probe the potentials of such visitation and to spur those who are seeking peaceful means to avoid a nuclear war that would make much of the earth uninhabitable. In this they are working through advisors to presidents and other rulers, for they have ready access to minds that are open to the possibility of averting bloodshed. And not just in the Western world. They are also active at this time in Russia, as the world will learn after the present leadership there falls and men feel free to discuss the reasons for that collapse, which is in the not too distant future."

According to the Guides, it would not be the first time that extraterrestrials have helped to re-seed the earth after catastrophic events have drastically reduced our population.

This book, then, will offer a survey of the various means by which extraterrestrials are said to be communicating with us, and provide specific examples of those who have seemingly been in touch with them, or are themselves from other galaxies. The Guides say that this interchange is slowly but surely leading us toward a more enlightened age, when peace shall reign on earth.

As I said in the beginning, I am merely a reporter of these alleged happenings, because I have yet to be honored by an unearthly visitation. But I can hope, can't I?

CHAPTER ONE

Unidentified Flying Objects

THE exciting new field of UFOlogy has created its own heroes, brave leaders who are willing to risk their enviable reputations for a cause in which they firmly believe.

Just as Dr. J. B. Rhine was the trailblazer who awakened the world of academia to the respectability of ESP research, so Dr. J. Allen Hynek and Dr. R. Leo Sprinkle are the pathfinders who have established the credibility of enquiry into the widespread UFO phenomenon. All three men brought impeccable credentials from the scientific and academic communities to their chosen task. All earned Ph.D. degrees, and all have had to endure "the slings and arrows" of their colleagues.

Dr. Rhine, director of the parapsychology laboratory at Duke University until his retirement some years ago, became its most famous faculty member despite the barbs of his peers.

Dr. Hynek, Emeritus Professor and Chairman of the Department of Astronomy at Northwestern University, was selected by the U.S. Air Force as its chief scientific consultant to Project Blue Book, the government-financed UFO investigation of the late 1960s, because of his towering reputation and his strongly skeptical attitude toward the spate of "flying saucer" reports. But unlike the discredited Condon committee report emerging from that inquiry, which brushed the matter under the table, Dr. Hynek studied the evidence and became so convinced of the reality of the sightings that he established a Center for UFO Studies (CUFOS) in Evanston, Illinois, which he has headed since 1973.

Dr. Sprinkle is a psychologist and Professor of Counseling Services at the University of Wyoming at Laramie, where each summer since 1980 he conducts the Rocky Mountain Conference on UFO Investigation that attracts "contactees" from around the world, although he is required by the university to divorce his interest in UFOs from his academic activities.

The two lines of enquiry do not overlap or tread on each other's toes. Dr. Hynek and his organization concentrate their efforts on establishing the physical actuality of alien spacecraft that are observed and/or visited by earthlings, encouraging the reporting of all such sightings and dispatching investigators to the scene of the activity.

Dr. Sprinkle's interest centers more on the "inner man," with emphasis on the psychological changes and physical manifestations that occur in humans who believe that they have been UFO abductees or contactees, and who under hypnosis seemingly recall minute details of these encounters that were mysteriously blocked from their conscious awareness.

There is little doubt in the minds of those who have seriously looked into UFO phenomena of the past few decades that the United States government has deliberately engaged in a massive cover-up. According to investigator Richard Sigismond, a contributing editor to *International UFO Reporter,* the magazine published by Dr. Hynek's Center for UFO Studies, our top-level National Security Agency has in its files a minimum of 131 top-secret documents on the subject of UFOs, "which it refuses to release because of national security." He adds that it requires "little mental effort to conclude that NSA would hardly waste its time preparing 131 top-secret documents on a subject not worthy of attention, scientific or otherwise."

Sigismond was hired by Dr. Edward U. Condon and his right-hand man, Professor Robert Low, to the staff of Project Blue Book in 1967, but he quickly resigned after a private interview with Dr. Condon, during which he says that he came to believe that this highly regarded scientist was not seriously interested in engaging the UFO subject. Resignations also were handed in by several committee members, including Mary Louise Armstrong, Dr. Condon's chief administrative assistant.

But sometimes citizens are far ahead of their government, which sponsored that cover-up. A Gallup poll concludes that some fifteen million Americans claim to have seen UFOs, and that more than half of our population believes that UFOs are "for real." Each issue of the *International UFO Reporter* is replete with eyewitness accounts of UFO activity and of the subsequent investigations conducted by experienced UFOlogists who have found definite evidence: circles of scorched grass where a mysterious craft has landed, electrical blackouts, snapshots taken of UFOs, multiple witnesses to a single event, and other convincing data. Some of the witnesses are highly trained technicians, airline pilots, chief meteorologists at airports, and law enforcement officers. Others are simply ordinary people who encounter extraordinary phenomena. Or as Dr. Hynek characterizes the reports, "They are incredible stories told by credible people."

Dr. Hynek's chief assistant is John Timmerman of Lima, Ohio, a Cornell University graduate in sociology, who in the early 1950s was an investigator for Project A, a group established by the engineering faculty of Ohio Northern University to check out UFO sightings. Timmerman became so impressed with the obvious integrity of the witnesses that he subsequently threw in his lot with Dr. Hynek. With the assistance of a highly sophisticated computer at the University of Illinois, they are currently comparing the similiarities of 110,000 cases of UFO encounters which should add greatly to our present knowledge.

The innumerable sightings described in any given issue of Dr. Hynek's magazine originate in practically every geographical area, but the events are surprisingly similar. Those who report the incident are driving along a lonely stretch of road at night, when their car engines suddenly stop, and after a missing gap in time, of which they have no recall, they are able to proceed. Or they are awakened at night by a brilliant light shining through their bedroom window, they go outside to investigate, but remember nothing else until morning. Or they and their companions are on a highway, when their attention is drawn to an object in the sky that speeds faster than jet planes, suddenly stops and noiselessly hovers over them, then takes off with alarming suddenness, makes a complete right (or U) turn, and vanishes into the light of the moon, or the sun if the viewing occurred in daylight.

In the January 1984 issue, under the title "A Cosmic Watergate?" Dr. Hynek details innumerable, and thrilling military aircraft encounters with UFOs, the bottling up of these events by government agencies, including the National Security Agency, and the frustrating attempts to win release of the documents through the Freedom of Information Act. Larry Fawcett, a former law enforcement official who had his own encounter with UFOs, requested these reports on behalf of CAUS (Citizens Against UFO Secrecy), carried his fight through the courts, and was finally given copies of some documents with line after line heavily blacked out, so that the material contained therein was indecipherable.

Commenting on this censorship, Dr. Hynek said he can personally attest to the "unspoken embarrassment that pervaded" the U.S. Air Force Project Blue Book, and its eventual dismissal of the UFO phenomenon. "Clearly it would be bad public relations for the air force to admit there were things going on in the air over which they claim mastery, which were potentially frightening and over which they could exercise no control," he said. "Far better to dismiss the whole thing as public hysteria, hallucinations, IFOs, and even as subversive propaganda than to admit openly that they had a problem that needed study and solution. So, following Pentagon guidelines, Project Blue Book officers did their best to downplay UFO reports that were puzzling and to publicize those many UFO reports that could easily be explained and which, therefore, were not UFO reports in the first place. Time and again I witnessed deliberate attempts to withhold from the media information about 'good' UFO reports, and the distribution of ad hoc explanations for puzzling cases to get the media off their back.''

Dr. Hynek sees two great mysteries in UFOlogy. The first is: What are UFOs? What lies behind the thoughts of "incredible tales from credible people"? The second mystery is: Why the apathy to the UFO phenomenon from the scientific community? He says of this: "One would think that the scientific world would be agog, furiously curious and anxious for answers, when highly credible people such as military and commercial pilots, ships' officers, engineers, law enforcement officers, technicians and public servants in high places report UFOs. But no! Where is that much-lauded scientific curiosity that we are taught in school?''

Searching for answers to his own questions, he says there would seem to be two related, deep-seated reasons for UFO apathy. "One might be called the 'stepladder' effect in the acceptance of new ideas," he mused. "Suppose our present understanding of the world about us is thought of as one of the rungs of a ladder. When something new comes along which is just a step or two above this rung, it is not difficult for us to make the small transition upward. But let something come along which is many, many rungs above our present level of understanding, then the human mind rebels at the transition. The jump to the higher rung is just too great. That would be like asking the best minds of Galileo's day to seriously consider nuclear energy.

"Asking us today to accept the elusive presence among us of manifestations of some form of intelligence other than our own, to which the very best-documented UFO reports unmistakably point, is asking us to jump to a precariously high rung on the ladder. It is not a matter of lack of evidence. It is a lack of the *kind* of evidence our present position on the ladder demands. It demands a piece of a UFO, a landing on the White House lawn, a cosmic petition presented to the United Nations. Lacking these, the UFO phenomenon is dismissed as inadmissible on the present playing field of science. But where is the scientific curiosity about why such UFO reports should not only exist, but persist over the years?

"A second reason for UFO apathy is the fear of the unknown. Our minds feel safe and comfortable on the lower rung of the ladder. Let us not be disturbed from our cozy, comfortable intellectual position. Let us not think about things that, deep down, disturb and frighten us. The power of the human mind to close its doors to the unwanted, the unknown, and the fear of the 'too strange' has been attested to all through history, especially in the history of science. It is apparent today in the reluctance to accept the reality of the UFO phenomenon."

To carry Dr. Hynek's analogy of the ladder and our resistance to unprovable facts a step further, how many of our grandparents would have embraced the idea that within their own lifetimes, men would walk on the moon? Yet our astronauts landed there on July 20, 1969, and by means of television that was beamed into our living rooms called it "One giant leap for mankind."

A growing but still small number of scientists are

beginning now to take an interest in the UFOs, which seem to be arriving in all shapes and sizes, from the more familiar saucer-discs to the recently widespread sightings of boomerang-shaped craft. The remainder of the scientists must be reincarnations of those who once clung to the lower rungs of the ladder and persisted in believing that the earth not only was flat, but also the center of the universe.

Dr. Hynek and his organization receive numerous reports from trained investigators throughout the world and, not surprisingly, the pictures they sketch of the objects seen and the space people allegedly observed are nearly identical with those drawn by American contactees. It is a worldwide phenomenon, but so many articles and books have been written about the physical manifestation of these unidentified flying objects that I will leave that subject to those who are more qualified than I, through personal investigation, to lay the facts before the people and their unheeding governments.

To me, the most interesting aspect is the remarkable effect that UFOs and our space friends are having on earthlings with whom they have apparently been in contact.

CHAPTER TWO

Channelers and Abductees

U NLIKE Dr. J. Allen Hynek, who was originally enlisted in the investigation of UFOs because of his doubt of the phenomenon, Dr. R. Leo Sprinkle began his own research because of personal encounters that had gradually changed him "from a scoffer, to a skeptic, to a believer in the reality of UFO phenomena." He frankly admits, therefore, that his work may be biased, but in light of scientific apathy and governmental cover-up, how else does a doctor of philosophy become interested in probing such an offbeat subject?

Dr. Sprinkle relates that in the fall of 1949 he and a fellow student, Joe Waggoner, "watched a flying saucer, or Daylight Disc, moving over the campus" of the University of Colorado at Boulder. They discussed their experience with each other, but not with others, because until then they believed that "only kooks see UFOs." He did, however, begin to wonder about an observation that he could not explain.

Seven years elapsed before he experienced another sighting. He had meanwhile graduated from college, completed a four-year stint with the armed forces, returned to Boulder and enrolled in graduate school. Then, one summer evening in 1956 while he and his wife were driving to Boulder from Denver, they spotted an unusually brilliant red star, but realized that it could not be a star when it suddenly began to move between them and the Flatirons (Rocky Mountain foothills). "We watched it for several minutes," he recalls. "It would hover, then move; hover, then move. It had no sound, and no features that I could observe, but I knew something unusual was going on because I could hear the honking of horns below us in Boulder. The object went north and finally disappeared from our sight. We expected to read a big story about the object in the next day's papers, but there was nothing."

This second experience convinced Dr. Sprinkle of the reality of UFOs, "whatever they might be," but he was unprepared for the next step. As a psychologist he had become adept at hypnosis, but when a colleague hypnotically regressed him to the fifth grade, Dr. Sprinkle saw himself aboard a spacecraft looking out at the stars. Beside him was a tall man who told him that he should learn to read and write well, so that when he was older he could help others to become aware of the purpose of life. That memory, like so many of those he was later able to awaken in his client-contactees, had apparently been blotted from his conscious mind, perhaps through some form of hypnotic suggestion made by space people aboard their craft.

After completing his doctoral studies in 1961 at the University of Missouri, Dr. Sprinkle had to endure the catcalls of his colleagues when he determined to pursue his interest in UFOs. He became a consultant to several organizations that were investigating the phenomenon and soon was being invited to participate in television panels that were interviewing alleged abductees or contactees. Dr. Sprinkle shared the questioning with such luminaries as Dr. Carl Sagan, Dr. Hynek and top-flight science writers, and he says that as a psychologist he was fascinated to observe that the so-called UFO abductees were not only highly intelligent, but as self-aware, sincere and open as the skeptical professors and writers who were asking the probing questions.

Having by now interviewed and/or hypnotically regressed over 250 contactees, Dr. Sprinkle finds that some of them are still hesitant to accept the validity of their experiences, which reminds him of the little old Irish lady who, when asked if she believed in ghosts, replied, "No, but they're there!" When asked if he truly believes in the existence of UFOs he grins and says, "No, but I've seen them."

As a result of his investigations, he has drawn the following composite of a typical abductee: He/she is driving in the country at night, sees a light that is moving strangely, and stops to observe it. To his relief the light darts away, and he resumes his journey, but on looking at his watch discovers that an unaccountable hour has elapsed. He begins to feel disoriented and wonders if he should discuss the incident, but for fear of being taunted decides to keep it to himself. Then he begins to have weird dreams about UFOs and space aliens. He may discover a strange scar on his body, as if a minor operation had been performed, or he suffers nausea or skin rash. Next comes the compulsion to visit libraries and book stores in order to read everything he can find about psychic phenomena and UFOs.

Ultimately he realizes that he must talk to someone who will understand his story, and he hears of Dr. Sprinkle. Under subsequent hypnosis, the typical abductee seemingly relives that missing hour of his life aboard a spaceship, sees himself being physically examined by space beings, and sometimes closely questioned about earth life through some sort of mental telepathy. The one constant is that all of the contactees have been altered by the mysterious encounter. Their attitude toward life and their personal interests dramatically change. They become what some have described as "cosmic citizens," feeling a part of the universal brotherhood and bored by the aimlessness of their familiar routine.

When Dr. Sprinkle inaugurated his summer conferences at Laramie in 1980, he had to use all of his persuasive powers to convince most of the contactees that they should "come out of the closet" and share their experiences with others. He defined the purpose of the conference as "an opportunity for UFO contactees and UFO investigators to become acquainted, and to share information about UFO experiences," but some insisted on anonymity, for fear of unwelcome notoriety. Since then, the annual conferences have steadily grown in numbers of participants—and in bravery. And contactees come from all over! In 1981 A. S. Husamuddin came from Kishna Giri, India, to describe a number of UFOs that he has witnessed there while in the company of family members and business associates, enumerating some of the sightings in precise detail. And Paul Norman, head of a UFO investigative group in Sydney, Australia, reported on an encounter with a UFO over Bass Strait by a pilot who radioed a description of the strange craft directly overhead. "Then his transmission ended," he concluded. "Neither he nor his craft has ever been found—no traces of anything."

Numerous Americans, giving their real names and addresses, have also related their encounters, but Dr. Sprinkle's most widely discussed hypnotic subject is Pat McGuire, a Wyoming rancher. Born to an Irish-Catholic family in 1942, he claims to have seen scores of UFOs at his ranch and to have been abducted by them at least twice. He first contacted Dr. Sprinkle in 1976 to report a number of sightings and also two cattle mutilations on his ranch. His original opinion was that "some sex cults from the university" were responsible for the mutilations, and he and his brother-in-law determined to "catch the guys." One evening they observed a "flying saucer" descend toward a ridge approximately two miles from McGuire's house. Through a telescope Pat watched the UFO as it hovered, then moved around the ridge. A cow, which had been under the UFO, was no longer there, and the next morning when Pat drove to the area he found a calf bawling, but no trace of the missing cow.

Later, under hypnosis, he "recalled" being transported some years earlier to an "oval room" for instructions by alien beings on where to dig a well. Thereafter he set up the rig and hired a driller to dig a well at the spot designated, while his relatives and neighbors jeered at the idea of water beneath the arid soil. At a depth of 350 feet he hit pay dirt. The well began pumping 8,000 gallons a minute of fresh water, which could irrigate 14,000 acres of malt barley, and although his chastened neighbors began putting down well shafts in the hope of tapping into the same underground source, they were unsuccessful.

In the years since then, numerous UFO investigators have visited the McGuire ranch, gazed in awe at the gushing well, and had encounters there with spacecraft and strange flashing lights. Dave Schultz, an electronics technician, has described a "loss of time" experience in 1980 while watching for UFOs on Pat McGuire's property. During a subsequent hypnosis session, according to Dr. Sprinkle, he recalled "memories of an abduction by UFOlks who somehow took Dave and two others on board a craft and probed their minds for information. Schultz gained the impression that the experience was a lesson to him in terms of personal growth and his wish to build a center for spiritual healing." Dr. Sprinkle also reports on three young men who came from California to camp on the ranch, hoping to have a close encounter and get a ride on a spaceship. They did experience sightings of UFOs, and a loss of time for which they could not account. But under hypnosis they described "memories of frightening encounters and a feeling that they had been told by UFOlks that they were not ready, mentally or spiritually, for space travel."

At this point I asked the Guides for some clarification. Why, if our space friends can materialize themselves here, do they bother to arrive sometimes in UFOs? And why do they occasionally engage in what would seem to be harassment of earthlings? The Guides said they would refer my questions to Algarr, "an old gentleman from Arcturus who has been eager to communicate" with me, and he wrote:

"Ruth, we sometimes use spaceships because of the gear that they can transport, to take people aboard, and also to take samplings of earth life, for we do not want it all to be destroyed when the shift of the earth on its axis occurs. These samples are reseeded on other planets, and so are some of the missing persons who have willingly come with us when our mission was explained. They are not kidnapped, if they do not wish to leave. But some do, including airline pilots and adventuresome young people. Pat McGuire did not need that one animal as much as we needed for it to be preserved, by stocking another planet. We are not thieves, but preservers of earth life in other spheres."

I have been in direct contact with several persons who submitted to hypnosis by Dr. Sprinkle in order to understand what has happened to them. Among these is Peggy Otis, then of Denver, Colorado, who told me that while driving herself and her young granddaughter, Jenifer, down a neighborhood street at 10:20 P.M. on October 14, 1978, she saw what she assumed to be an airplane. "It was massive," she recalls. "Sparks were being emitted from underneath it, and it suddenly came down so low that I thought it was going to smash the top of my car. I screamed at Jenifer to wake up, and jumped out of the car. The craft was dome shaped, and I could see someone moving inside it. We were terrified, thinking that it was going to crush us. Then I telepathically received the message, 'Don't forget us,' and it floated away, stop-

ping again over some houses on Broadway, and
then disappeared toward the moon. But at that
point two other UFOs floated between me and the
moon. Jenifer said she noticed a man and woman
in a red car looking up at the spaceship, but all I
remember was seeing it take off at top speed.

"Jenifer and I got back in the car and rushed
home to tell my husband, who is an engineer with
a scientific mind. We called the airport to ask if
anything strange had been sighted, but there was
nothing, even though the huge UFO had made a
humming sound that Jenifer said reminded her of a
disposal."

Under hypnosis Peggy relived her terror in minute detail, and described the man in the dome of
the spaceship as "white head, no ears, slanted
eyes, not over four feet tall, with his hands on
something like a steering wheel." She felt that he
was trying to draw her toward him, and that he
was telling her, "We'll be back. We love you.
Don't be afraid." She also had the impression that
she saw an airplane inside the dome of the huge
craft and wondered if it was a missing craft such as
the one that disappeared over Bass Strait in the
South Pacific.

And then what happened? Like so many other
contactees, Peggy developed a keen interest in the
psychic, and began holding development classes at
her house. She believed that she was "receiving
messages" to leave Denver because the climate
was bad for her health, and when her husband was
offered a job at Vandenberg Air Force base in
California they moved there, where she held weekly
classes "to try to raise the vibrations of the world."
They now live in Littleton, Colorado.

Among others of Dr. Sprinkle's hypnotic subjects with whom I have been in contact are Joseph and Carol Ostrom of Fort Collins, Colorado, who seemingly had separate encounters with space people before they met each other and married two years ago.

Carol, a graduate in horticultural science, says that her parents observed a UFO low over their house in Queens, New York, when she was about a year old, but refrained from telling her about it until she was grown. More recently she had an encounter ("a crash and a light—then no conscious recollection of events") while on a camping trip with a man and his son who claimed to be from Venus, and afterwards she "became aware" of what was in the minds of others before they spoke. Under hypnosis she apparently recalled several visits to spaceships, two of them before the age of five, in which she saw doctorlike beings and heard the words, "There is this biology experiment." Describing a dark-haired man with "colorless, intense eyes," she said, "It's a man's voice, smooth and rather deep. I hear it! But I don't ever see his mouth moving. He talks with his eyes. His head doesn't move, yet he looks straight at us at all times."

These impressions, and her description of other supposed visits could be put down to vivid dreams or imagination, except for the emotional response that they evoke. She says of this: "I have a personality trait of being tough, a female Mr. T; yet when the thought or discussion of being on a spaceship comes up, I begin to cry uncontrollably."

Her husband's encounters are more specific. In September 1978, after exploring a cave in the Catalina mountains, Joseph Ostrom and a friend were driving home to Tucson when, near Oracle, Arizona, they spotted two small orange-yellow lights in the darkness near the top of a farmhouse. At first they thought them to be an animal's eyes, "until the eyes moved away from each other and came to a dead halt over us. I could see that they were glowing orange with a reddish glow around the edges. The objects seemed to be circular in shape. Then they flew off quickly to the right in a zigzag, up and down fashion, the second light following the exact track of the first light, and they were suddenly gone."

Five months later, Joseph and his then wife were asleep in their third-floor hotel room in Ayia Galini, Crete, Greece, about 3 A.M. when he was awakened by a loud electrical humming and the howling and barking of dogs in the street below. His graphic description follows: "As I opened my eyes I was shocked to see the room filled with a reddish orange light. My first impression was that a transformer had exploded and the hotel was on fire. Awakening my wife, I jumped out of bed and ran to the balcony doors. The first set of doors was louvered and the second set was of glass. By the time I got the first set open the light was gone, but I could still hear the humming. When I got out to the balcony the sound seemed to be over the top of the hotel, but I couldn't see anything from that vantage point. I went in and talked to my wife about it, and then fell quickly asleep. I 'dreamed' that the door to our room opened, and an exceedingly tall man said he understood that I would be interested in coming with them. I asked if I could bring my camera, and after consulting someone he gently said no. I went with him into the hallway and up the stairs to the roof, where I could see the harbor and town below, and where a small gray disc hovered noiselessly above us. A turquoise-colored beam came down and paralyzed me, then lifted me up and into the craft. This craft took me to a larger craft where I was told that the world was in a sorry state, and that I was to help. I don't remember the rest of it, but the next morning I went up to the hotel roof, and it was exactly as I'd 'dreamed' it. I am now convinced that this was not a dream.''

Was it only a dream? If so, why did Joseph Ostrom's life begin to change so drastically? "Prior to that time I had been content to be a commercial artist," he muses. "I was very much involved in the world in a normal way, with very little concern for my spiritual life. Within months of that event I found that I was able to discern and evaluate the colors that I had been seeing in people's auras. I began to get more and more involved with metaphysical studies. I developed a method of drawing an ink portrait of a person, and after putting in the layers of their aura, psychically interpreting them. I began having dreams that vividly repeated the same message, which was a map of the continental United States. There were several black dots scattered across the country, and toward each of these dots lines of people were moving in single file, each person carrying a suitcase in his right hand. My own dot was at Fort Collins, Colorado. Within a month after these dreams I had closed down my advertising agency and was on the road to the great unknown in Fort Collins, leaving behind family and friends in Tucson. Since then many things have occurred, but the most monumental is a reacquaintance with the tall man whom I met on the island of Crete in those early morning hours. It came unexpectedly in the form of automatic writing on November 17, 1982, and our communications continue to this day, with his words proving of great benefit to those who have given me questions for him. He is presently helping us to build a chromosonic healing device. Color has become very important to me.''

Under hypnosis with Dr. Sprinkle, Joseph described the preliminary details as noted above, and then told of entering a larger mothership after his transferral from the smaller UFO. ''A dimly lit room, and it seems to be fairly empty,'' he began. ''The man takes me up an incline into a room with very high ceiling. The light is unusual. Feels very pleasant. There's a table against the walls, which are slanting. Someone is sitting at the table. A man with gray skin, long thin face, drawn looking. He doesn't look at me. The other man puts me on a chair, smiles, and says to relax and listen. An echoey voice says they are taking a desperate measure in contacting people; afraid for us, afraid for existence. I asked, Why me? And the voice said because I was accepting and had special talents to deliver the message to others. I asked a bunch of questions, like what about picking up leaders and scientists instead, and they say it's more powerful to pick up average people because ultimately they are the ones who will bring about change. They say that I saw them when I was very young, in northern Michigan in a cottage in the woods.

''Getting my questions answered was like receiving three months of information in a few hours. They say we can do this. We will learn soon how to use chromosonic physics to heal, to travel through time and space without resistance, to be in physical as well as other planes. They show me a chain or device for attuning physical and subtle body for healing. Attuning frequency of color and sound. A connection made for my eyes and brain and information. They say I have auric vision . . .''

The material became more technical, then he resumed: "We've come to a place where we go into another craft. A city. Large. It's beautiful, lots of people, some like me and some like ones I met earlier. All warm; heartfelt warmth, love. All seem to know me and I know them. Nobody says anything. Warmth is all that needs to be said. A skyway that opens to a giant shopping mall. Clothes of different colors, all one-piece outfits and boots. Lots of unusual plants, and they are warm and friendly, too. Shown lots of things. Rooms with educational centers, getting ready for large numbers of people. I will be going back there. OK, going into a room to sit in a chair, and doctors are going to look at me. I need to alter some things, control inner self, inner physical, improve health. They show me a movie of things to come. I have to go back. He has his arm on my shoulder and walks me to a dark room where we get on small ship. We go back to Crete and I get left on the roof and go back to my room. I think my physical body was still on the bed, but I'm not sure of that. In the morning I feel really good.''

Joseph Ostrom is by no means unique in believing that he is a channel through which space beings are sending messages for the benefit of humankind. Bizarre as it may seem to many of us, an impressive number of otherwise normal, workaday human beings consider themselves to be in frequent telepathic contact with the inhabitants of space fleets that are said to be continuously orbiting our planet. So numerous are these "receivers" that some of them have formed networks to share their information, and several have published booklets.

The most prolific of these channelers is Thelma Terrell of Durango, Colorado, better known to her wide following simply as Tuella, the "space name" assigned to her by the Ashtar Command, an intergalactic fleet that has allegedly been circling us in outer space for millennia. In several loose-leaf type books published by her Guardian Action Group, the best known of which is titled "Project: World Evacuation," Tuella presents urgent messages from "Commander Ashtar, the highest in authority for our hemisphere," and from such other formidable-sounding crew members as Hatonn, Lord Kuthumi, Monka and Andromeda Rex.

The chief import of that book's message seems to be that although most earthlings will lose their physical lives when the earth shifts on its axis at the close of this century, a goodly number of enlightened ones will be evacuated by the galactic fleets and returned to earth for its rehabilitation. Tuella quotes Andromeda Rex as follows: "The Great Evacuation will come upon the world very suddenly. The flash of emergency events will be as the lightning that flashes in the sky. Our rescue ships will be able to come in close enough in the twinkling of an eye to set the lifting beams in operation in a moment. Mankind will be lifted, levitated shall we say, by the beams from our smaller ships. These smaller craft will in turn taxi the persons to the larger ships overhead, higher in the atmosphere, where there is ample space and quarters and supplies for millions of people."

Since I am a perennial doubting Thomas, I was ready to dismiss Tuella's material out of hand, until my Guides declared that there is indeed an

intergalactic fleet above the earth, and that an evacuation of certain earthlings whose superior development will be required in the New Age is scheduled
to occur. "Tuella is definitely in touch with this
fleet that is circling the earth," the Guides flatly
asserted. "Her home constellation is Orion, but for
a long time she was one of the principal members
of the Ashtar Command and is able to contact
them directly. She came to earth to be the contact
between the fleet and the earthlings, because she
has often traveled in the fleet."

I protested that I was somewhat turned off by
some of her messages that purport to come from
Jesus, the Mother Mary and other saints, and the
Guides responded: "She would be wise not to in-
fuse so much Biblical religion into her messages,
as the Ashtar Command is nondenominational and
like all spacelings worships the one Creator of us
all. She is not actually hearing from the ones you
mention, but is feeling what they might have conveyed. We don't like to see the issue unduly tied in
with Biblical stories, for the worldwide appearance
of space people is not solely limited to those spiritual beings who have trod the earth, but includes
ones from other areas of space and other galaxies.
But make no mistake about it, Tuella is a highly
developed soul with an important mission for which
she volunteered."

In one of her newsletters called "Universal Network," Tuella includes a long message from one
she calls Soltec, who in discussing the work of the
galactic fleet among earthlings says in part: "In
this day the UFO movement has grown into a
higher plateau of understanding and awareness. In
the opening experiences of the movement there was
an emphasis upon a few who had outstanding reve-

lations and stories to tell, which was the necessary
approach for the times. Now the approach is through
the strivings of the soul in an [ethereal] sense rather
than a physical sense. This is why sightings in
general have lessened so drastically, along with the
hostility of your sky patrols. The nature of the
experiences of the early fifties was needful for the
awakening and attention-getting maneuvers to fulfill the mission of that day. The seed remained to
sprout anew in your day, but on a higher level of
manifestation. The thousands of cosmic telepathic
contacts of this day would have been impossible
without the forerunner activities of the earlier days.

"The spiritual contactee is now proving a thousand times more effective in the enfolding of light
and understanding in the quiet ways than the ex-
ploited physical contactees of the past ever could
be. Now the changes are coming from within and
working outward rather than the former process in
reverse."

Another woman who claims to channel messages
from outer space is Diane Tessman of Poway, California. A former school teacher who publishes a
monthly newsletter called "Star Network Heart-
line," she has written about her experiences in a
booklet called *The Transformation*. She calls her
unearthly source Tibus and identifies him as follows: "He is a member of the Free Federation of
Planets, a member of the Ashtar Command, and
has visited earth many times throughout the ages.
He is not a 'popular' Space Brother to channel,
such as Monka or Andromeda Rex. As far as I
know, Tibus channels only through me, and I have
not so far been able to channel any of the other
Space Brothers."

Certainly, when Dr. Sprinkle hypnotized her three

years ago, to heighten her recall of UFO contacts, Diane provided one of his most interesting transcripts. The Idaho-born woman first described several childhood memories of being taken aboard space shuttles and conveyed to a mothership, where she met Tibus and two doctorlike beings who seemed to be performing medical experiments on her body. Asked if they were humanlike, she replied: "One was and one wasn't; it was more insect looking—humanoid build, large eyes. I wasn't supposed to observe too closely." Throughout the session Diane repeatedly broke into sobs, and Dr. Sprinkle commented that it was as if the recall of these events was "felt from the very core of her being, from her soul itself."

Diane has what appears to be a clean surgical scar between her nose and upper lip, which she has had since the age of three, although her mother cannot account for it. Diane believes that it was caused by surgery performed on a star ship, and that laser "needles" were used to reach the brain, "going back of the nose" to implant a replica of Tibus' soul in her. When I asked the Guides about this seemingly remote possibility, they replied that an operation was performed on her aboard the spaceship as a child, but that it was "an experiment on her face, not her brain." Diane's booklet also describes visual encounters that she has had in recent years with UFOs, both in Florida and California.

I asked the Guides for any further comment on the alleged "channeling" by such individuals as Tuella and Diane, and they replied: "You should stress that space people are indeed able to contact through mental telepathy those who are open in their vibrations and take time for meditation, which is the way to hear the unspoken words. The contact is real, Ruth.''

Well, how are we to know whether telepathic communication is less valid than the spoken word? How are we to know whether out-of-body travel in or out of spaceships is less real than physical travel? Why are the lives of those who have seemingly had encounters with UFOs and space beings so dramatically altered, even if they cannot recall these events except under hypnosis? Do UFOs exist only in that mysterious fourth dimension, or are they actually viewed and touched in our three-dimensional world of matter?

I do not know. But Dr. Sprinkle reminds that in a 1979 lecture in Brasilia, Brazil, Dr. J. Allen Hynek said that theoretical physicists have long been confronted with the dilemma of light. It can be viewed as ''reacting like particles,'' and it can be viewed as ''reacting like waves.'' And Dr. Hynek posed the question: If the physicist can accept the dilemma of light-as-particles and light-as-waves, then cannot the UFO investigator equally accept the dilemma of UFOs-as-objects and UFOs-as-psychic events?

Certainly many UFOs, though not all of them, have been simultaneously viewed by a number of witnesses and have left telltale physical evidence of their landings on the ground.

CHAPTER THREE

Contactees

A MIND-EXPANDING correspondence commenced in February of 1983 when a fan letter arrived from Joyce Updike, a housewife in Ovid, Colorado, who has spent all of her adult years as a bookkeeper, while also rearing a family of seven children. Unlike most of those "fans" who wanted to know if they were Walk-ins, or to be told their mission in life, Joyce sought to awaken my interest in extraterrestrials and to understand the "whys" of her own unsought experiences with space beings.

She writes with engaging frankness, down-to-earth wisdom, and delightful flashes of humor that brighten my day. In that first of many letters she said in part: "Whenever I read your books I know deep within me that what your Unseen Friends have told you is truth. I use your books as 'required reading' for my six grown children, to help keep their feet on the ground and their heads in the clouds at the same time. Your Guides have fully explained almost everything I need to know for soul growth, but they touch lightly the subject of UFOs. You seem slightly interested in the subject, but somewhat withdrawn. I am well aware of the stigma attached to open display of interest in the extraterrestrial field. It is fashionable to see the movie *E.T.* as long as one categorizes E.T. along with Mickey Mouse.''

Although I have not seen that famous movie, her reference made me smile as I read on: ''There are thousands of us in your reading audience called 'contactees.' Most of us only call each other 'contactees.' The rest of the world knows us as John Smith's wife, or the sixth-grade teacher, the new diesel mechanic, the psychology professor, or the newspaper editor. Once in a while a person who has been 'contacted' will be interviewed by a pulp newspaper (the weekly type). The paper will sensationalize their report, make them feel like fools, and cause them to doubt their sanity. Because of this some businesses are ruined, some marriages fail, children are ridiculed at school, jobs are lost. Even through all this, the 'contactees' hold to their stories and begin to look for people like themselves, so they can continue to function in society. We tell each other our stories, try to find similar experiences, openly discuss our lives and ask each other, 'Why me?' and 'Where do we go from here?' Our numbers continue to grow.

''I will tell you one of my experiences, because I need to understand it better. Perhaps your Guides can help. Under hypnosis I saw myself aboard a craft, on an examining table. Two entities were approaching me with tubes attached to an instrument panel at the side of the craft. My head was in something that resembled a microwave oven. I have only heard this particular experience described by one other person, a guest on the David Susskind show, who related a similar occurrence and said she was told that an extraterrestrial named Antron would be occupying her body.''

Joyce said that on reading *Strangers Among Us* the first time she was interested, and believed it, but after being "prompted" to reread it she stared at herself in the mirror and asked, "What now?" At that point she mentally heard something say, "Your name is Yarbah. You are to finish this life and then begin a new one."

Naturally I was intrigued. A small-town book-keeper in rural Colorado could have had no normal means of knowing it, yet since finishing work on *Threshold to Tomorrow* the Guides had been pressing me to write a book about extraterrestrials, and had been dictating reams of unwanted (by me) material on how and why extraterrestrials are allegedly arriving now in such large numbers. Actually I was hearing much less about UFO sightings lately than in previous decades, but the Guides insisted that the space people have found new and quieter means of entry to earth. I therefore wrote to Joyce, asking if she could describe her supposed encounter in more detail, and she replied that there had apparently been more than one.

She then wrote as follows: "I experienced a UFO sighting in 1967 when I was thirty-five years old. Until then I knew nothing of UFOs except that those who saw them were said to be viewing swamp gas, or the planet Venus. Since there are no swamps in this area of Colorado, and the planet

Venus has never been reported to land in a farm-
yard, I believe I saw a UFO. I was washing the
cupboards at 2 A.M. one August morning in 1967. It
was necessary for me to do my housework at night,
because I worked away from home and had seven
children who manufactured dust and lint just by
walking across a floor. My cupboard doors were
varnished wood. Suddenly they glistened so brightly
I couldn't see to wash them. I looked out the
window to see where so much light was coming
from. The entire yard was filled with light, resembling that of welding torches. It was too bright to
look at, and I couldn't see the boundaries of the
light, which was patterned blue and white-white. I
became very frightened. I am an extremely protective mother, but I did not even check on my seven
children to make certain they were safe. I simply
put out the lights, locked the door and went to bed.
Frankly, I never did believe that I could behave
that way. I awakened refreshed before 7 A.M., fully
clothed atop the bed covers, and only mentioned
the lights in a joking manner at breakfast. But the
incident didn't end with my lighthearted dismissal.
Thereafter my interests changed. I had always loved
historical novels, but I stopped reading fiction and
began reading occult science—anything about UFOs,
ESP, psychic development, reincarnation, ancient
mysteries, Atlantis, Egyptology, pyramids, and ancient religions.

"My long, healthy head of hair began to fall out,
and I wore a hair piece at the top of my head for
two years. Several times my eyes, and the eyes of
my two-year-old daughter would redden, burn, and
ooze mucus. Sixteen years later my hair is still thin
and dry, and my eyes require artificial tear drops
each morning. My daughter wears photogray glasses.

Poltergeist activity became common in our house. Lights would go on and off, knickknacks would tumble from shelves, ashtrays would fly across the room, articles would disappear and then be found in some comical place. Some of the children developed sudden psychic abilities. One daughter would announce that someone was hurt, and shortly we would hear an ambulance siren. Another daughter had two out-of-body experiences while at school. The 'baby' talked of past lives. I began receiving words, phrases and messages telepathically, through some sort of mental process, from an unidentified source. Some of the words were new to me, and when I couldn't find them in my old abridged dictionary, my eldest daughter found them in the college library: words like seismology, antimony and telemetry. Remember, this was in rural Colorado.''

The years passed, and the mental messages persisted, although Joyce said that she desperately tried to shut them out. Then, while watching a television program in 1980 she learned of R. Leo Sprinkle, Ph.D., a psychology professor at the University of Wyoming who was interviewing, and sometimes hypnotizing, abductees or contactees who had witnessed UFOs. Accompanied by a son-in-law who had seen a UFO in the sky over New Mexico, Joyce went to Laramie, Wyoming, to consult Dr. Sprinkle.

Under hypnosis, she began telling him about an incident that seemingly occurred circa 1959 in North Platte, Nebraska, where she was then living. She saw herself waiting beside a country road to greet two men wearing space suits, headgear like old-style diving helmets, and thick-soled shoes. She was feeling happy to see them "again." One space man was holding two metal rods that were aimed toward her, while the other climbed over a barbed-wire fence, and she wondered why he didn't simply float over it. She could see their spaceship half-hidden behind a hill.

Now Joyce continues: "At that point Dr. Sprinkle asked me how I was dressed, and I almost lost the scene because I didn't want to tell him that I was in my housedress and apron, and had driven the car to that rendezvous while barefoot. He then asked me to describe the craft, and I found myself inside it on an examining table. Two men were standing at one side of the room. They appeared to have removed their bubble helmets and simply wore winged-type skull caps. Their bodies appeared well formed, neither excessively short nor tall, although I could not recall their faces in any detail. Another man on the opposite side of the room was dressed in a surgical garment, three-piece and loose fitting, and a hood with a smoked glass window over his eyes. He was standing before a circular, glass-covered instrument panel wearing gauntlet gloves with pointed, pincher-type clamps at the end of the thumb and index finger. This man approached me and raised my right arm by the elbow. Then I woke up, and consciously I knew nothing of this encounter."

Dr. Sprinkle rehypnotized her, and directed her to go to the sighting outside her kitchen window in 1967. After reliving the conscious sighting, as described earlier, she told of floating through a tunnel of light that was "semisolid like cotton candy, being on an examining table with my head in an ovenlike contraption, two men standing by my right side, one holding a small black book like a pocket Testament. Another entity was above my head. Two other men approached me carrying hoses with

round-ball metal ends, and I woke up. I knew that
this spaceship was more commodious than the previous one I'd visited, and that I didn't like these
men very well. During the next hypnotic session I
saw myself looking through a window of the spaceship while we were moving rapidly and low over
the countryside. That is all that Dr. Sprinkle could
get me to recount, and he said he gained the impression that I had promised 'someone' not to disclose
further information until my children were all
grown.''

Joyce, describing herself as ''a stubborn woman
concerned with proper behavior,'' says she probably would withhold some kinds of information even
under hypnosis, but has no idea what she may
have blocked out. She says that when she told her
husband, after hearing Dr. Sprinkle on television,
that she intended to investigate the sighting that
had haunted her since 1967, he admitted for the
first time that he had seen a large circle of scorched
grass near the barn, around the time that she saw
the bright light there. It had not occurred to her to
search the grounds the next morning.

She told me that since her sessions with Dr.
Sprinkle she is calmer and stronger, and that she
''finally got up enough courage to leave my husband, after years of trying to patch up a weak
marriage.'' But according to Joyce, strange occurrences continued to beset her and her children.
''Sometimes my body was so charged with electricity that a female co-worker refused to stand
next to me, because her polyester pantsuit would
wrap around her legs. I could make a length of
thread dance and rise in the air by waving my hand
over it. I cannot wear a wristwatch, because it
stops and starts. Information is being given to me

telepathically, at home and at work. My twenty-nine-year-old daughter awoke one morning recently on her living-room couch, dressed in her wedding dress, which wasn't at all wrinkled and didn't appear to have been slept in. She found two marks on her left arm similar to intravenous feeding marks. She had gone to sleep in her own bedroom as usual, and remembered nothing of having changed into the wedding dress."

Two months ago Joyce's youngest daughter, aged sixteen, told her that someone invisible kept touching her on the arm. "That same night," Joyce said, "someone invisible sat at the foot of my bed. The bed depressed and creaked at its sitting and raised when it stood. I have felt very real taps on my shoulder, only to turn my head to see no one standing there. I had some wind chimes in my kitchen a year ago, and one evening they began to sway and chime. There was no draft or sudden movement near them. I tried to recreate their movement by waving my hand and walking rapidly past them, even turning up the heat to see if the forced air furnace would do that. They stayed motionless."

At the beginning of my correspondence with Joyce Updike, I naturally asked the Guides about her, and they wrote: "She is a superior being who in previous lifetimes has assisted others to find themselves and look within. In ancient Greece she was a priestess of the Temple of Diana, and in others a teacher and prophet. She was selected for contact by space beings because of her high development and her understanding of the interplay between various cultures in past lives."

That explanation satisfied me for a while. Then I asked again, and they wrote: "Joyce is one of those rare ones who speak forthrightly, are sensi-

ble, down-to-earth, keenly aware of the lighter side
of life and the very sheer curtain that separates
earthlings from the rest of humanity in the cosmic
beyond."

So far, so good, but, my curiosity getting the
better of me, I finally asked if Joyce came from
another star or planet like some of the others about
whom the Guides had informed me. I laughed aloud
when I read their response, which began: "Thought
you'd never ask!" They then continued more so-
berly: "She is from Sirius and was a highly developed soul before entering the body of the farm
woman after the contact with the spaceship that
she does not consciously remember. They [those
on the spaceship] did not bring her in, so to speak,
but opened the way for her predecessor to yield to
the soul who wished to enter and take on the
chores of a large family, in order to experience
earth life at its fullest, and perhaps at its hardest.
She is a star Walk-in with a fountain of wisdom
flowing in and through her, and is well worth serious handling in the book."

If true, then like so many others who have been
contacting me, Joyce is both an earthling and a
spaceling, having enjoyed continuing existence both
on this planet and in other galactic systems.

Since 1981 Joyce has been happily married to
her second husband, Hal Updike, an affable truck
driver who took a relaxed view of her alleged encounters with space beings when she "confessed"
to them shortly before their marriage. His work
necessitates frequent absences from home, and during those lonely evenings Joyce has utilized the
time to try to develop mental contact with space

beings. After reading somewhere that one should request communication with a specific individual in space, she asked during her regular 9 P.M. meditation to be put in touch with "Hatonn, the Record Keeper of the Intergalactic Fleet or Space Command or Whatever." She said she had forgotten his exact title, but that she did indeed make telepathic contact with a being who told her that her husband would have an encounter "very soon" with a spaceship. Then the being signed off with the clearly received words, "This is Hatonn of the Intergalactic Fleet or Space Command or Whatever. You see, we enjoy a good laugh, too."

This communication occurred in July 1983, and when Joyce excitedly wrote to me about the "promise" that Hal would have a sighting or encounter, she added: "This is great news. Now I can share all my life with Hal, without excluding this portion of it." Wondering how she could endure the waiting period, she laughingly wrote that she's the kind of person who prays, "Dear God, grant me patience and give it to me right now." In wondering why women usually have contact with space people at home, whereas men encounter them while in automobiles, she whimsically wrote: "Perhaps even the Space Brothers have heard about women drivers."

Joyce wrote that Hatonn had been trying to teach her out-of-body travel during meditation, with no success, and that he finally told her to relax; that they would work with her when she was asleep. The next morning her daughter Lilli asked, "Did Hal come home last night?" Joyce said that he had not, whereupon Lilli responded, "I heard noises from your bedroom and people walking, about five o'clock this morning. And I brought your purse in from the porch.''

In her letter, Joyce commented to me: "The female psyche, again! Even when I leave for an early morning space ride, I apparently take my purse.'' She also said that the space friends had indicated a willingness to help her find the half sister she had never seen, who had been given out for adoption before Joyce was born. Just recently she wrote to tell me that after clues to her whereabouts seemed to fall into her hands, the half sister was located in California. They had just had a joyful reunion, and were delighted to learn that both had "read Ruth Montgomery's books and were both interested in UFOs.''

To return to the letter of July 1983, ten days after receiving it I had another one from Joyce, jubilantly announcing that Hal had indeed had an encounter, in which he personally flew the spacecraft for a time, and that he holds a pilot's license. She said she had not previously told him that Hatonn had promised an encounter for Hal, so that his experience had nothing to do with the power of suggeston, or expectation. Hal Updike subsequently wrote out for me every detail that he could recall of the spectacular adventure. The following duplicates his own handwritten account:

The following incident occurred while I was laid over in Flagstaff, Arizona, on July 30–31, 1983. I will attempt to put it into writing while the details are fresh in my mind. I will not try to color [the experience] or mislead anyone reading this, either toward fact or fiction, so you can draw your own conclusions.

I had delivered a load of 2 × 8 lumber from Escalante, Utah, to Winslow, Arizona, on a Saturday, and was successful in getting unloaded on this Saturday afternoon, which is very unusual. After unloading, I questioned the young man who ran the forklift about a sawmill in Winslow that might have a load going out of that town. He said they'd been working two shifts at a place called Duke City Sawmills and might have a load going out. I went over there, but found the office locked and no one around. I found an excellent restaurant, with reasonable prices and parking facilities for my big truck, and after enjoying the food and atmosphere I proceeded to Flagstaff, Arizona, and parked my truck at the Little America Truck Stop. I listened to the radio for awhile, and at about 7:40 P.M. local time I decided to retire for the night, even though it was still light outside. I slept fairly well (in my truck sleeper) until at 3:53 I was awakened by some sound and a bright light shining into the southeast end of my sleeper. I sleepily thought it was the sun, but eventually realized that the sun would not be shining at 3:53 A.M. in Flagstaff, Arizona.

I felt as though I had just drifted back to sleep when I had the sensation of being lifted. This feeling lasted only a matter of seconds. Then I felt as O. J. Simpson would have felt had the Hertz rental car commercial been real and he was floating into the driver's seat of a car. However, I was being placed in the pilot's seat behind the controls of a large aircraft of some sort. I observed a man of about twenty-seven or twenty-eight years to my right, who appeared to be my co-pilot. A young lady of about the same age was to my left, about three feet behind me, and facing as though looking out the window, and away from my left shoulder. There were instruments and controls in front of her, as though she must be the navigator charting the flight of the craft. She appeared to be much fairer in complexion than my co-pilot, she having rather blond hair, and he with very dark hair. I was told somehow that I was to call him Jock. I believe that this was done through thought communication, since I recall no verbal contact at this time.

For some unknown reason there seemed to be some argumentive state of disarray in the passenger section of the craft. The craft seemed to be cylindrical in shape, like a large elongated balloon. I remember thinking that it flew much the same way; however I had excellent control over the craft, and of course I do have a pilot's license. It began to become clearer that the argument behind me had something to do with the fact that some of the passengers wanted to depart from the craft in the area over which we were then flying. I seemed to be flying the craft at about 50 to 60 miles per hour, and kept it about 1500 to 2000 feet above the ground surface.

I felt that this area must be that of southern Colorado or northern New Mexico. The quarreling passengers were told that they could depart by some means of parachute with which they were outfitted. Approximately ten of them did depart in this manner. I could look down and see them floating to earth with ease, the tops of their chutes looking like pinkish-orange designer paraphernalia of some sort. I then speeded the craft to a much higher speed, taking only a matter of minutes be-

fore I observed a lush valley of farmland. There were mountains both to the west and east, the ranges running in a northwest to southeasterly direction. I landed the craft facing in a southerly direction, and I remember thinking how easily the balloon-shaped craft maneuvered and floated to earth.

It seemed that hours and hours passed before anything further occurred. I seemed to be in charge of the craft, but some other force was feeding me thoughts or orders about what to do next. At this point Jock and I departed the ship with some type of suits on. They appeared to be silky, white, and very comfortable while we were outside the ship. As we departed the craft on the east side, at about the center of it, I began to call Jock my lieutenant. We made our way to the rear of the craft in a northerly direction, and as we made our way around to its west side I observed snow about six inches deep. There were footprints near the craft, which seemed to have melted the snow almost to bare ground.

As Lieutenant Jock and I made our way to the front of the craft we observed a lad of about fifteen or sixteen, who appeared to be a local farm boy, and very curious about the craft that had landed in his domain. The young man was ordered aboard ship, where he was to be questioned by myself, since I spoke his language. There were no weapons in evidence, but the young man and I both knew that he must follow orders or there would be enormous danger to him, and possibly to anyone else who disobeyed the wishes of the remaining passengers aboard the craft. Lieutenant Jock, myself and the young farm boy then entered the craft from an entrance just to the left of the cockpit where I had been seated to fly and to land the ship.

As soon as we entered the ship I became very uncomfortable with my white suit on, and had to take it off immediately. Through the thought process I again was ordered to question the farm boy about the surrounding area and what might be available to the members of the craft. I was not told exactly what they were looking for. I remember thinking that the boy had a lot of gray hair in his dark hair for a lad of his age. He was dressed in a short-sleeved, horizontally striped shirt, the narrow stripes of purple, yellow and white. He wore glasses at times. I looked at his shoes, which were the tennis type, and his pants were a faded-blue crushed denim.

At this time I feel that I should describe the remainder of the individuals who were aboard the craft. In addition to my lieutenant, Jock, and the young lady navigator there was a young couple of about thirty to thirty-two years. They appeared to be rather carefree, yet very happy to be with each other and to have arrived at this landing spot, as if they had completed a very long journey and it was now over. There was also a middle-aged couple who also appeared affectionate to each other and happy that their journey was over. The man, however, seemed more forceful, and I felt that perhaps he was the one who was feeding me the thoughts and orders at all times. There was also an older man, around eighty, who seemed rather sickly. He had silver hair, and wore a maroon shirt.

Toward the end of the questioning of the boy, he asked where we were from, and I was dumbfounded because I did not know. There was a pause of a few seconds, and as I recall, the only verbal response I heard from any member of the craft was when three of them spoke at one time. It sounded as though one answered Theroxen, and another said Therogin, while the third said something like Theaubedeaux. I wondered if this could be a galaxy, a planet, a continent, a state or county, or if each was from a different city.

At this time I was left to guard the young farm boy, with no weapon, and it seemed like hours passed. I did not know where any of the individuals aboard the ship had gone. The farm lad explained to me that he had told us everything he knew, and that he would be missed if he didn't return home, and that others would come looking for him. Since I had no actual weapon, or means of stopping him other than physical force, and since I felt that he was stating the truth I turned my back on him, facing the passenger compartment, and when I turned back the boy was gone.

It seemed only a short time until the group returned, with no sound. They were just there. The middle-aged man seemed very upset with me for letting the boy go, and I tried to explain through thought process that others would come looking for him, and he was of no further use anyway. All aboard, except for the middle-aged man, seemed to agree with me, and I could see a look come over his face as if I had also served my usefulness to them.

I could again feel the sense of weightlessness, and felt myself floating. I awoke in the sleeper of my truck at about 8:15 A.M. with mixed feelings, because I felt that I had not completely fulfilled my usefulness to them. However, I also felt that I was not sure that I was ready to commit myself to eternity with them.

As I write this, I am filled with questions to which I do not have the answers. Was I actually beamed aboard a spacecraft to fly this ship to their destination? Why was I chosen? What happened to the original pilot? Were Lieutenant Jock and the lady also beamed aboard to help them in their quest? I hated to leave them, because I liked them very much, especially Jock. What happened to the ones who parachuted out at the beginning? How many of these individuals were aliens, and how many earthly beings? Did they fulfill their quest? Did they stay, or did they leave? Will they requisition someone else to fly their craft, or will I again be called? Or was this all a dream? I cannot explain it, but as I finish writing this report my entire body is shaking uncontrollably.

Those were better questions than I could formulate, but when I put them to the Guides they merely wrote, "Hal's experience was real. He was indeed aboard a spaceship for some time, and is strengthened by the event." A few days later, puzzled by their seeming reticence, I asked the Guides: "Are you saying that Hal Updike's experience was a physical reality, not a dream? Are the UFO encounters real in the sense that they are in the three-dimensional world, or in the fourth dimension?"

With their usual patience, they replied: "They are in the three-dimensional plane, for the contactees actually see and touch the spaceships and even the occupants, but they are in a sense fourth dimensional in that most conversations are conducted through thought transferral." I willingly left it at that, until a year later when I was typing out Hal's handwritten account for this book. Then, restimulated by his graphic description, I again asked the Guides to comment on Hal's adventure. Was he beamed up there? Did he dream it? Was he there only mentally, or did he participate physically, in a physical spacecraft?

This is their startling response: "It was a physical experience, and the spacecraft existed in the third dimension, having been recreated in earth's atmosphere after leaving the mothership aloft. He was taken from his bed in the truck sleeper in a dissolved state that you earthlings do not understand, but put aloft in the pilot's seat where he did indeed guide the ship and experience what he truthfully recalls. He was in physical form while in the ship, and again when he awakened, and throughout, except for the brief periods of removal from and return to the sleeper. It is a matter of altered state that spacelings thoroughly understand, for since all is energy they know how to alter the vibrational patterns and manipulate the atoms."

In completing this chapter, I had two more queries for the Guides. Was Hal, like his wife, from another galaxy? And why did not Joyce consciously recall her two visits (or more) to spaceships? My Unseen Friends replied that Hal came here from a star within the constellation Hydra, and that I was not to worry about "exact names and places, because there are millions of stars in the firmament, and to earthlings it is like wanting to know the name of someone in a previous lifetime ten or fifteen centuries ago, when that name is unknown to earthly records nowadays."

"As to Joyce," they declared, "she does not remember because she promised not to discuss it for a time, and was told that the events would be erased from her conscious mind. That promise was fulfilled, and she is now free to speak of it as much as she likes."

They said that no similar promise was exacted from Hal Updike, and that he is consequently able to recall his adventure in remarkable detail. It could fairly be assumed from this, therefore, that our space friends are now ready for us to know that they are here.

CHAPTER FOUR

Walk-ins From Sirius

SIRIUS, the heavenly body that the Guides identified as the previous abode of Joyce Updike, apparently possesses qualities that develop some highly unusual personalities. Known as the Dog Star, in the constellation Canis Major, it is the brightest star in the firmament, and more than twenty times as luminous as our own sun.

During the course of writing this book, the Guides specifically named two other individuals who, they said, had sojourned on Sirius between earth lives, and who returned directly from there, this time as Walk-ins. Certainly to me, at least, their remarkable talents seem "unearthly," so let us consider these cases separately.

Charlotte King of Sacramento, California, is a

human seismograph. Far more accurately than any of our advanced scientific devices, she is able to detect impending earthquakes and volcanic eruptions, specify the time of the disaster, and pinpoint the locale. She can also, while blindfolded, correctly ascertain faults in the earth's crust so that precautions may be taken.

She has repeatedly demonstrated this ability to the bafflement of geologists and other scientists, having been thoroughly tested by physicists at the U.S. Environmental Protection Agency, as well as by scientists at the U.S. Government Bureau of Standards, the Neurology Health Center in Portland, the Western Thermographic Laboratory in California, the Institute of Applied Physiology and Medicine in Seattle, and the Sacramento State University in California.

Charlotte has predicted the exact dates and time of all the recent eruptions of Mount St. Helens, besides some three hundred California earthquakes since 1979. Official government records kept on her predictions reveal 85 percent accuracy on earthquakes and 100 percent on volcanic activity worldwide.

Dr. Frank Yatsu, chairman of the Neurology Department at the University of Texas School of Medicine, has surmised that she hears noises generated by the earth itself, adding: "Charlotte may be detecting shifts in the earth's electromagnetic field, which may also affect certain animals and cause them to behave in an unusual manner, a phenomenon long under serious study in Russia and China."

A number of the scientists who have tested Charlotte conclude that she hears in a very low frequency range ordinarily unavailable to human ears.

She explains that there are a series of seven tones varying in pitch, frequency and rhythm that she has learned to associate with seismic activity in specific geographical areas. She has also learned through study and observation that when a particular tone increases in volume or overlaps another tone, a seismic event will occur within twelve, thirty-six or seventy-two hours, depending on the intensity of the tone.

Unfortunately it is not tone changes alone that trigger her awareness of approaching seismic activity. A great deal of pain is associated with the phenomenon, to the extent that she is unable to hold regular employment because she is so frequently ill, and is often hospitalized. These symptoms in head, chest and stomach indicate to her the area where seismic activity is shortly to occur, and the severity and type of quake or eruption.

When Charlotte, who had read some of my books in the psychic field, called me in September 1984 to discuss her peculiar and inconvenient talent, she expressed the belief that it was "some kind of karmic punishment" for deeds that she may have committed on the legendary continent of Atlantis many thousands of years ago.

Intrigued by her story, I sought counsel with my Guides, who declared: "Charlotte King came into that body as a Walk-in from Sirius about eight years ago, when she found that the occupant of a particularly sensitive body wanted to leave, and that this body would work well for her in her mission to warn earthlings of imminent disasters and give them time to evacuate dangerous areas, if they wanted to survive in their present bodies. She is not quite the phenomenon that you believe, for there are others throughout the world with similar gifts of sensing earth changes and alterations beneath the earth's crust. Hers is not a karmic indebtedness, but a divinely given ability to help others, through her alerts."

When I passed this message along to Charlotte, of whom I had never previously read or heard, she was impressed by the Guides' far-ranging knowledge. It was true, she said, that there are others with a like gift, and also true that she had been rescued from a suicide attempt eight years ago. Recounting the circumstances, she said that on Christmas Day in 1976, jobless and separated from her husband, she was feeling such emotional and physical stress that she began gulping wine, and found a half-full bottle of pain pills. "I decided to take them all," she recalls. "I just wanted out, to end the emotional and physical pain caused by the constant sounds that I was hearing—sounds like foghorns that no one else could hear."

She said that she reached the hospital too late to have her stomach pumped out, but after sixteen hours in intensive care she suddenly roused and "became aware that I did not want to die. I knew I had a job to do, that my kids still needed me and my marriage could be salvaged."

It was apparently during that period that the "old" Charlotte, also a sensitive, departed and the "new" replacement came from Sirius to alert earthlings to the radical changes that were beginning to occur on planet earth. The Walk-in Charlotte did put the marriage back together for a while, but it eventually was dissolved, and she asked me about a particular man who has been supportive of her endeavors in more recent years.

I put her question to the Guides, who reported: "Charlotte is doing exactly what she volunteered to come in to do. She was on Atlantis shortly before the breakup of that continent into smaller islands and knew from experience precisely what the sounds were like before the catastrophes there. In Atlantis, she was the wife of the man she mentions, and they were well matched there; he helped her to alert others to escape from dangerous areas that were shortly going beneath the sea."

Asked about her childhood in this lifetime, Charlotte said that it was an "average" one: "I was raised on a small farm, with two brothers and a sister. According to my mother and an aunt, until the age of two years I used to scream every time I heard a low or vibratory sound such as a train whistle, or water going down the drain. I'm told there were also times when I would drop my toys, turn my head and listen, but no one else could hear anything. I sighted my first UFO with my family in 1950 near Salem, Oregon. All I remember was my parents telling me that it kept pace with our car, and that the airport also saw it but did not know what it was."

Now thirty-eight years old, Charlotte says that the foghornlike noises that she began hearing in 1976 "caused so much trouble in my marriage, because no one else could hear them, that after three months I filed for divorce." To determine whether the noises were psychic, she enrolled in a parapsychology class at the local college, and discovered that she "knew things about the pyramids and their energies that were simply not in the books." Then came the suicide attempt that apparently resulted in the substitution of egos.

Shortly thereafter, the "new" Charlotte determined to search in earnest for the causes and sources of the sound and the pain that no one around her was experiencing. A professor at Oregon State University came to her residence and was able by electronics to record the signals that she was receiving. She also had hearing tests in a specially equipped booth and learned that although most people could hear at the 20 to 32 dB range of sound, she heard sounds in the 7 to 10 dB range.

In early 1979 she began reporting changes in sound to a Portland, Oregon, television station, and seventy-two hours later a quake would occur. "The stronger the sound, the larger the quake," she says, "and the TV people concurred that I was correct sixty out of sixty times. Then on June 23 I awakened at 2 A.M. with a feeling of real fear. The sound was louder than I ever remembered and was definitely different. Later I learned that at about the same time there began a forty-eight-hour beaching of sperm whales on the Oregon coast at Florence. Forty-one large mammals died as a result of being crushed by their own body weight on shore. I believed the whales beached because they were not getting back the same echoes they were sending out; they became confused and beached. I passed this information on to the scientists who were studying their death, but they did not believe me. Two days later four quakes of moderate intensity occurred in Big Bear, California. One year later a newspaper article said the scientists now believed the whales beached because their sonar was being jammed by the approaching quakes, so due to the loss of forty-one beautiful sea creatures I was able to put the sound and effect together."

Soon afterwards, Charlotte discovered that she would suffer severe physical pain and sharp sound effects a day or two before large quakes in such faraway places as Japan and Italy, and after they occurred the symptoms would pass. By then the scientific community was taking keen interest in this human seismograph. Scientific laboratories began in-depth testing of her strange ability, and after she accurately predicted the first eruption of Mount St. Helens in March 1980, and its massive later eruption May 18, national television networks and magazines beat a path to her door.

"The Charlotte King effect," as scientists now call it, is the prime subject of an on-going study called Project Migraine that is being conducted by Christopher Dodge, a life science specialist with the Library of Congress in Washington, D.C., whom she telephones each time that she experiences the familiar symptoms, and pinpoints where the quake or eruption will occur.

Dodge, who has a master of science degree from George Washington University, told me there is "very compelling evidence" that certain people like Charlotte are actually tuning in to the earth's electromagnetic field and experiencing a geomagnetic effect. As a specialist in electromagnetic field biology, he had for some time before meeting Charlotte been collecting "fascinating anecdotal material" about the advance reaction of animals to impending earthquakes, and he sees no reason why humans should not be able to duplicate the feat. "And it's a lot easier to work with humans than with animals," he added with a grin, "because people can talk."

He said that he became interested in launching Project Migraine after the U.S. Senate Committee on Science and Transportation asked him to undertake a research study into biological earthquake predictions. "I first made contact with Charlotte King in February 1981," he recalls. "She had approached the Library of Congress to seek assistance in identifying those factors that might be responsible for her hearing sensations. I was so impressed with her sincerity and her record of accuracy that I decided to monitor her supposedly premonitory sensations on a formal basis, to determine whether her claims were valid. Since a common denominator of these sensations is severe headaches, we both decided that the study should be called Project Migraine."

Dodge set up the project as an independent undertaking apart from his governmental activities, and has since located a dozen other individuals who seem to share Charlotte's remarkable talents. He then established a telephone message system so that at the first warning signs these sensitives can call in to record their symptoms and make their predictions on timed tape, for official verification. He says that the combined batting average for the group is seven or eight, on a scale of one to ten.

"One of our subjects is a woman in New York City, the noisiest electromagnetic center imaginable," he declares, "but she is particularly accurate about Italian earthquakes. She nails them every time. My role is to coordinate the predictions of these sensitives and run the verification, and we're beating the meteorologists at their own game. Some of my own friends in that department say they come to work each morning and flip a coin to predict the weather, but we're right on the button."

Asked about Charlotte's batting average, Dodge said that her performance has defied all expectations. "She has been 100 percent accurate on Mount St. Helens and other volcano activity, and over 80 percent right on earthquakes, when even 60 percent would have been remarkable.

"I look at this subject with the cold, fishy eye of a biologist," he continued, "and I'm convinced that just as some animals can give advance warning of seismic activity, so can certain humans. Some people try to classify this ability as psychic—a precognitive factor—and although I believe in leaving all doors open until we know more about the psi factor, I'm convinced that it's an actual ability to respond to geomagnetic effects, particularly since the thirteen people I've studied at close range seem to have similar reactions, at the same time, in advance of a quake of five-or-above on the Richter scale."

Dodge said that after experiencing pain for some hours or days beforehand, a common denominator is that shortly before the actual quake the pain leaves, and there's a euphoric feeling. "That's what I call the 'Oh-oh Effect,' " he added. "It means watch out, because the quake is imminent."

Dodge then gave me a fascinating account of a personal experience that he shared with Charlotte King. "Remember when there was to be a planetary alignment on March 10, 1982?" he began. "And the prophets of gloom and doom were predicting a dire occurrence on that date? Well, the newspapers and TV stations asked me to make a prediction, but I refused because Charlotte was exhibiting no symptoms of anything out of the ordinary. I happened to be in California at that time, and the alignment day passed peaceably. It was, in fact, unusually quiet in the seismographic field. The next day, however, Charlotte became violently ill, and because her symptoms for volcanic activity are different and give an earlier lead time than for earthquakes, we made a prediction that Mount St. Helens would erupt on the afternoon of March 19. We also notified seismologists at the U.S. Geological Survey and at the Volcano Center in Vancouver. As the time approached, although official instruments were showing no activity, television cameras were posted outside Charlotte's house, and reporters milled around. At exactly 7:30 P.M. Mount St. Helens erupted with a bang, and Charlotte was vindicated again.''

How could she do it? How could she know that it would be eight days off, and not hours or weeks? I put the question to Dodge, who replied: ''From experience. Having memorized the signals, such as the frequency of her headaches and the rumblings in her ears, she is able to pinpoint the location and the time, as well as the severity of the upcoming event.''

Charlotte herself says of the warning signs: ''The sensations change according to what the event is going to be. Steam bursts from a volcano are announced by a building pressure in my temples and ears. An earthquake in the volcano is preceded by pain in the center of my forehead. A series of four tones that cut off sharply means seismic activity in northern California. Southern California is a series of tones that fade out slowly. A vibrational effect means the quake will occur in the ocean, or under water. Kidney problems, breaking capillaries and heart spasms also seem to tie directly into the seismograph.''

Two years ago, while lecturing before a college psychology class, Charlotte began having severe stomach pains ''that felt like hard labor.'' When they failed to lessen, she was taken to a hospital for examination, but no physical cause could be ascertained. Shortly thereafter a series of earth-quakes occurred in the Sierra Mountains, her pains ceased, and she now knows to associate "labor pains" with the Sierras, and to predict the time and place of the ensuing quakes.

In October 1984 she telephoned to say that she had now learned to identify a new symptom with another specific area. "I call it seismic flu," she confided. "It occurs only when an earthquake will occur in granite, and since the only granite in this part of the country is in the Idaho and Lake Isabel areas, I've been predicting those quakes almost to the minute."

Certainly the seismologists and television personnel whom she regularly alerts when her various symptoms begin are no longer scoffing. They all remember too well her telephone call of May 17, 1980, when she was violently ill and bleeding under the skin. "Mount St. Helens will erupt in twelve hours," she declared. In exactly twelve hours and twelve minutes the volcano blew its top, killing a large number of people who might have been forewarned to clear the area.

Charlotte believes that hers is a "teachable ability" that others can learn, but given the disastrous effect on her health and the frequency of pain, how many of us would volunteer for such a thankless project? The Guides have said that she "volunteered" to enter as a Walk-in from Sirius in order to help alert earthlings to the dangers facing this planet during these two decades. The United States Government is baffled, intrigued, and sometimes embarrassed by her amazing accuracy. After all, Uncle Sam is expending millions of our tax dollars annually to support seismographic equipment and pay the salaries of scientists who monitor the stations, while Charlotte, who far exceeds their accuracy, lives virtually in want.

Perhaps there is more fair play on Sirius than on earth!

In a last attempt to understand why anyone would willingly volunteer for such a life of service, I asked the Guides to tell me what Sirius is like. Their response was this: "The star Sirius is a training station for those who are going on to other planets, or returning to their own planets for special projects. It is a good place to test one's mettle and utilize the lessons that one has learned. Those returning from Sirius have strong motivation and a willingness to sacrifice themselves for the good of humanity."

The other person whom the Guides identified as a Walk-in from Sirius is David Paladin, an old friend to readers of *Threshold to Tomorrow*. A noted artist who now lives in Albuquerque, New Mexico, with his wife, Lynda, he was born on a Navajo reservation in Arizona, the son of a white missionary father and Navajo Indian mother. David had exhibited few abilities other than a talent for running away from home until the outbreak of World War II, when the wayward lad who had jumped ship in the South Pacific was hustled into uniform, given some training in cartography and shipped to Europe with the Office of Strategic Services (OSS), forerunner of the CIA.

In Germany, while mapping installations behind enemy lines, he was captured and thrown into a Nazi prison camp where he was grilled, beaten, starved and left for dead by retreating Germans. Advancing British troops found 120 abandoned bodies, and tossed them into a boxcar for removal from Germany for burial, but in searching them for identification noticed a faint stir of life in one of them.

As a spy for the United States, David had worn a German uniform without identification, and after being sent to a British field hospital in Vienna, Austria, he remained in deep coma. Because he occasionally mumbled in Russian, he was then transferred to a hospital for Eastern European refugees, where he remained until fingerprints eventually identified him as a "missing and presumed dead" American soldier. Still in coma he was sent to an Army transport hospital in Battle Creek, Michigan, where after two and a half years he at last regained consciousness. Asked his name, he promptly replied, "I'm an artist. My name is Vasili Kandinski."

That sounded sane enough, except for two conflicts: His fingerprints tallied with those of David Paladin; and Kandinski, the Russian artist who is the idol of abstractionist painters, had died in France at the age of seventy-eight in 1944, when David would have been eighteen. To further complicate matters, as David became more alert he admitted that he had never heard of Kandinski and knew no Russian until he heard himself speaking it.

The convalescing soldier asked the Red Cross for art supplies, and promptly began to execute sweeping abstracts that caught the attention of the art world and were favorably compared with the paintings of Kandinski in style and symbolism. The rest of David's fascinating story is detailed in my previous book, but the Indian boy with only a sixth-grade education now teaches at universities, conducts workshops and seminars in the parapsychology field, and continues to produce remarkable paintings that some critics feel surpass those

of Kandinski. Several years ago, the Guides identified David to me as the Walk-in soul of the famous
Russian artist. More recently, when he confided to
me that he has had contact with space beings, I
asked the Guides for comment and they wrote:
"David is a highly developed soul who comes from
Sirius, a planetary system where those who have
completed their earth cycles go to learn how they
may further serve humanity." They then related a
curious story. Kandinski in later life, they asserted,
had also been a Walk-in from Sirius, and when the
soul who is now called David Paladin was no longer
able to keep that artist's body alive "he briefly
returned to Sirius and then found the body of the
soldier that he was able to revive for his work,
which is concerned with the preparation of earthlings for the New Age. He needed a body which
would serve him in a setting where he could do the
most good. That was in the body of an American
with Indian roots."

Puzzled, because I had not previously heard of a
case of two successive Walk-in appearances, I
asked: "Was David in Sirius during that long period of coma, or before?" My Guides calmly replied: "In both cases. He returned to revive the
body from death, but spent most of the intervening
time (of coma) on Sirius, until ready to resume an
active earth life in a well-functioning body. Not
hard to comprehend if you realize that such highly
developed souls are in and out of earth lives quite
easily, since they have mastered certain secrets as
yet unknown to humankind."

This whetted my interest to such an extent that I
telephoned to ask David if he would be willing to
tell me about his experiences with the space people
to whom he had fleetingly referred. David obliged

with the following report: "For four consecutive
nights in September 1961, my four-year-old son
claimed that he was being visited by a 'person'
named Itan who came into the house, awakened
him and took him into a big 'sky car' which he
claimed landed behind our house in the Granite
Dells area of Prescott, Arizona. I paid little attention, believing it to be a childish fantasy. My attitude changed when my next-door neighbor, a forest
ranger, told me on the third morning that he had
seen a flying saucer hovering over the area the
night before. He also claimed to have seen my son,
accompanied by a tall, thin man dressed in white
overalls, walking toward a strange greenish light in
the rocky area behind our house. He said that he
had called out to them, but then 'seemed to forget'
the incident until he saw me emptying the garbage
the next morning.

"We went into the house and talked to my son,
asking what he remembered. He said that he had
gone for a ride in the 'sky car,' going to where the
earth looked like a little dot. He said that they
brought him home and went into the garage, where
Itan and a friend of his 'milked' the truck that my
neighbor had parked there. We trooped out to the
garage and my son pointed to the oil drain plug,
telling us that was where they had 'milked' the
truck. We checked the oil level to find it showing
empty. On checking the oil plug we discovered it
to be loose, but there was no trace of oil on the
ground.

"We considered reporting the incident to the
sheriff, but decided that we would appear to be
fools. We did discover that there had been numerous reports of flying saucer activity in the area for
the past several days. Thereafter, on several occa-

sions my little son took my neighbor and me outside to point out different stars, naming them correctly. To us that was amazing, because the child had not been exposed to astronomy.

"Two months later I awakened one night to see a tall, rather thin humanoid form standing at the foot of my bed. He appeared to be wearing a one-piece silver-white jump suit. I sat up to make certain I was awake. He identified himself as Itan, my son's friend, and the conversation must have been telepathic, as I do not remember speaking aloud.

"Itan informed me that he and his friends were from another planet that existed in another dimension. They had visited earth for centuries and had attempted to make some contact with humans, but found most of them to be too manipulative and selfish, causing his group to limit their visits. He claimed that they had removed some 'genetic blocks' from some humans in order to communicate and share concepts that could be of some use to humankind. He indicated that they would never interfere with humankind's destiny, but would 'manifest' as humans periodically in order to 'plant seeds' for positive human growth. During the ensuing years there were numerous opportunities provided to draw upon the many gifts so openly shared by our space friends with Lynda and me, and our lives have been enriched as our desire to work toward a healing of the planet has intensified.

"Some years after that initial visit from Itan, I appealed for help in a medical emergency and was telepathically instructed to drive from Prescott to Albuquerque to meet a medical doctor who, according to my mysterious source, would be able to assist me. I drove to Albuquerque, half expecting to find that my information was an illusion, but upon arrival I did find the doctor. He was working on cancer research and was with a government agency. Even though he was quite abrupt, almost to the point of rudeness, he was able to provide the much-needed assistance. My source told me that he was 'manifested' as a human being for the purpose of providing humankind with a few new concepts in the field of medicine. I was informed that on occasion our space friends do take on a human identity, appearing with proper documentation, and finding ways to 'plant seeds' that may help us develop beyond our present limitations.

"The doctor 'manifest' is now in Germany, active in research and also in the peace movement, and openly sharing concepts for others to accept or reject. There are many others like him. I only hope that people will listen to those concepts and learn how to serve humankind better and to care for the welfare of the planet."

I asked David if he is aware of any further identity for his space friends, and he replied: "They identify themselves collectively as 'Kantarians.' They are 'interdimensional' beings, rather than beings from our own space-time continuum. Their guidance of our race goes back to its early beginnings. They are devoted to helping us without direct intervention, because they were at one time instrumental in helping us through a past cataclysmic period, and they had mixed with us genetically. I was informed that some humans are more responsive to them as a result of our own evolutionary growth. Some of us have fewer 'genetic blocks' to our awareness, which allows us to communicate with them. This kind of communication helps us better to serve humankind."

Are the Kantarians engaged in an eventual rescue mission?

I put the question to David, and he responded: "While they would be willing to assure our biological survival in the case of a natural cataclysmic period, they would leave us to find our own destiny. Should we outgrow our tendency to be exploitive, judgmental and manipulative, they could consider a more active partnership with us in our desires to reach the stars. My friends have insisted that we must accept the ultimate responsibility for our own fate as a species of beings. They would not prevent us from destroying ourselves. Only in the case of a natural cataclysm would they directly reach out to help. Then they would withdraw to allow us to utilize the concepts they have shared for our ultimate growth or destruction."

Eager to know more about the Kantarians, I asked the Guides whether they, like the Ashtar Command, have a circling fleet above us. This is their reply: "The Kantarians came from Sirius, as did David Paladin. It is a remarkable star in that it gives free rein to development of all talents that are usable for the common good, and the Kantarians are indeed protectors of their people on the planet earth, with whom they had early ties. Their fleet is smaller than the Ashtar group, but equally dedicated to helping earthlings. Impossible to say now how many will be taken off the earth before the shift, as it depends in large measure on the willingness of those there to leave the earth and go into orbit, and also to how many at that time will deserve rescue. The Kantarians will be helping with the alerts and assisting in rescue to some extent, although the Ashtar Command will be in charge of the actual rescue mission."

As if in benediction, David Paladin sent me a personal message that he said his space friends had asked him to deliver. "Dear Sister," it began. "The concepts you share with others may well lead to a humanity that openly explores and celebrates its creativity, recognizing that the loving creative spirit is indeed the same as the Holy Spirit of your Scriptures. It is our hope that humankind will listen to their inner voices and seek creative solutions to the problems that exist today, to build a spiritual and moral foundation that will become their true heritage. Like a phoenix, it will rise from the ashes of any cataclysm that might threaten your planet. Even a cataclysm can be a great opportunity for change and growth. However, the seeds for that growth must be planted now."

The message was signed: "Itan and friends, the Kantarian Confederation."

I had completed this chapter when it occurred to me that I had not told David that the Guides say he is from Sirius. What if he objected to being so categorized? I hastily sent off a note, and by return mail came his warm response. As a matter of fact, he declared, for the past couple of years he has been painting a number of Sirius works with such titles as "The Dream Crystals of Sirius," and "Song of Sirius." And he added: "I have also been drawn to other Sirius people."

Coincidence, do you think? I doubt it!

CHAPTER FIVE

Close Encounters

MY Guides have repeatedly stressed that spaceships are nonessential for the conveyance of spacelings to earth. These highly developed entities, they insist, are able to reassemble the atoms of their bodies within our atmosphere so that they become visible, physical beings, and can as easily disassemble the atoms when they wish to disappear. If true, it may be the only logical explanation for the cases that I will now relate.

Because the Center for UFO Studies (CUFOS) is principally concerned with physical evidence of UFO sightings and landings, Dr. J. Allen Hynek and John P. Timmerman referred to me a letter received in January 1982 from a man named Robert Hurlburt, who was then residing in Starke, Florida. They thought that the Hurlburt case might be more in my line than theirs, since no UFO was involved and I had recently published two books about Walk-ins.

Unfortunately, a number of years had elapsed since the alleged encounter, a frustrating circumstance in so many of the reports received at CUFOS headquarters, either because the participants had originally feared ridicule, or were unaware that a legitimate clearing house existed to investigate their claims. Hurlburt's letter proved so engrossing, however, that I began a correspondence with him and eventually made a number of long-distance calls to his relatives and friends.

Now in his mid-thirties, Hurlburt identifies himself as a commercial artist with a master's degree in art. But in July 1971 he was still residing with his parents in Claremont, New Hampshire, when he and his German Shepherd dog, Misty, set forth on an extensive hiking trip into the Green Mountains of Vermont. His intriguing first letter, somewhat shortened in the interest of space, describes what happened next.

"On our fourth day out, we came across a young man sitting beside a stream. It seemed to me unusual to find him in such a desolate area, as I noted that he had no backpack or provisions. He appeared to be in his mid-twenties, with straight, collar-length brown hair, rather slender, and slightly over six feet tall. He looked up as we approached and said 'good day' in what sounded like a British accent. Misty ran over to him readily, her tail wagging in greeting, which was unusual behavior for her, as she tended to be wary of strangers; but her enthusiasm led me to think this person was OK.

"I sat down beside him and asked if he had a

campsite nearby, to which he replied that he didn't.
I became suspicious at this remark, as we were
thirty miles from the nearest town. I asked how
long he had been in the area, to which he replied
three days. I asked myself, 'What the hell has he
been eating in the past three days, pinecones?' My
next reaction was that he might be an escapee from
Waterbury Asylum thirty miles away. He noticed
the. 44 magnum revolver at my hip and inquired
why I was carrying a gun. I told him that since
being attacked by bears in Alaska two years prior,
I now carried a gun when hiking in deep woods.
This explanation seemed to relax him, but not me.
Thinking that I was in the middle of nowhere with
some nut from the funny farm, I gathered my gear
and headed back toward the trail. As I was walking
away he called after me and asked if he might walk
with me for a ways. Reluctantly, I agreed.

"That day we walked sixteen miles, mostly up-
hill. I was sweating and out of breath, and decided
to make camp for the night. I noted that my companion wasn't even affected by our long, arduous
hike, which led me to believe that he was in better
physical condition than he appeared to be. As dusk
was approaching, I pitched my tent and gathered
some wood for a fire. My companion merely squat-
ted nearby on the ground, gently scratching Misty
behind the ear. He had told me earlier that his
name was John. I cooked us up a meal from my
provisions, and afterward brought out a bottle of
wine, pouring us each a paper cup full, and then
several more. I became rather giddy and rambled
on about myself, but he didn't seem in the least
affected by the wine. Except for admitting that he
had lived in England for a time, he seemed reluc-

tant to talk about himself, so we fell into silence after awhile.

"He noticed me gazing up at the stars and moon and asked if I thought there were other beings on some of those planets. I stated that I believed there were many civilizations on other planets, and that I thought those people had been visiting earth for centuries. He said, 'Would you believe me if I told you that I was from one of those planets?' That remark definitely blew it as far as I was concerned. My suspicions about him returned. I thought, 'This guy really is some nut that's escaped from the asylum. Maybe he's going to kill me.'

"I figured that it was best to try humoring him, so I asked which one he was from. He said you can't see it from here because it's so far away from earth. At my 'Oh, yeah' reply he said, 'You don't believe me, do you?' I said I didn't, and he replied, 'What if I showed you some proof that I am?' I asked to see proof, and he dug into his pocket and produced a whitish-colored stone about two and a half inches in length, somewhat oval in shape. It looked like a piece of quartz to me, so I asked, 'What's that?' He said, 'It's a communication disc that I use to keep in contact with my people.' I tell you, I was getting paranoid listening to that crazy kind of talk. I asked him how it worked and he said, 'It draws power from the life source of your body and directs it in a beam back to my planet.' I asked what in the hell he meant by life source, and he said, 'This disc absorbs the energy emitted from your body and then transmits this energy into a beam similar to radio waves.'

"I was getting more scared of this character by the minute. I asked if I could see the stone and he handed it to me. It seemed warm to the touch and I got a tingling sensation that ran up my arm into my head, like a chill, except warm. I held it up to the firelight but could not see through it, nor did it have any identifiable markings. It was just smooth and warm. John went on to tell me about this planet that he claimed to be from: that it was a warm, temperate planet with abundant flora and fauna; the atmosphere had a thick cloud cover and consisted of a high quantity of nitrogen, with oxygen and traces of other gases, some of them familiar to earth, some not. He stated that this planet had two moons and traveled in an elliptical orbit around its sun; and he told me its name, but I can neither pronounce nor write it. He said it was slightly larger than earth, had two polar caps, and a total population of around 500,000,000; that population control was strictly adhered to, meaning reproduction was not a haphazard occurrence; that there were seventy major centers of population; that there was no pollution or disease; [the inhabitants had] a life expectancy of 160 years; that a central committee of seventy representatives controlled the government and each member was elected by one of the seventy major cities by electoral vote of the populace; that there was no crime or famine, and everyone worked in unity to assist one another. The primary concerns of the people were scientific achievement, research and study of alien cultures, and bringing peace to all cultures. They had begun space exploration over twenty centuries ago. Their space vehicles varied in size and shape and were capable of speeds exceeding the speed of light, and were powered by drawing energy directly from the sun. He stated that his culture had been sent to earth to study us and someday to share its technology with us, but as yet we were not prepared to handle such power. He referred to us as infantile.

"I sat listening to all this in a semihypnotic state. I was overwhelmed by all that he'd said and was even beginning to believe him. He continued talking, all the while holding the disc between thumb and index finger, and stated that he was only permitted to tell me certain things; that when he had told me enough the disc would warn him by blinking on and off three times. And sure enough, that disc distinctly blinked on and off three times. It surprised the hell out of me. I asked if he'd been in contact with any other people on earth, and he said he'd met a young lady in my hometown and had told her about himself.

"I slept soundly that night and awakened at the break of dawn. My companion was gone! There was no sign of him anywhere, almost as if he'd never really been there. I cut my hiking trip short and returned home."

Hurlburt said that by means of a telephone directory he was able to locate and talk face-to-face with the young woman whom John had mentioned, and that she readily admitted knowing the space man, but added that she was not permitted to say much about it, and had not been in communication with him for more than a year. When he saw her again two years later, he said that she did not even broach the subject of John, but she had changed. "Before she was joyful and happy," he mused. "When I last saw her she was quiet and solemn, as though she was keeping some inner secret to herself."

After making several long-distance telephone calls, I was able to trace and talk with the young woman, who is now married and living in a different state;

but when I asked her about John and the mysterious stone she adamantly insisted that she did not know what I was talking about. Other remarks that she made verified what Hurlburt had written to me, but on the subject of John there was a closed wall.

That circumstance might have cooled my interest in the story, except for the changes that Hurlburt reported within himself since the strange encounter. He says that he has been affected "psychologically, spiritually, psychically and physiologically," but that the latter is the most evident.

"I maintain an average body temperature of only 96 degrees," he reports, "and I no longer catch colds or flu; my hearing and eyesight have become more acute, and I can perceive a broader spectrum of visual responses. But perhaps the most remarkable physiological change is that I have not aged at all since the experience, which leads me to believe that my metabolic rate has slowed down.

"Prior to my experience, my theological beliefs bordered on agnosticism, but since then I have come to accept a deeper understanding of what we call the creative force, and can now recognize that there are various manifestations of that 'force' existent on both a material and a subliminal level. The psychic aspects occurring as a result of my experience have been more subtle and intermittent than the other changes. Nevertheless I feel that I have obtained heightened psychic capabilities, although I cannot seem fully to master them. Sometimes I can see into other persons' heads and know what they are thinking or are going to say, and at other times I can 'touch' certain persons' minds and make them say certain things and act certain ways. Precognitive thoughts sometimes manifest themselves, but these too are uncontrollable.

"Thus, I can only say that I have indeed been 'touched' by a higher life form and know within myself that I have been given a message to deliver and a task to perform. What this message is, and this task, I do not know, as the full implications have not been made known to me as yet."

I asked the Guides for comment on that strange encounter in the Green Mountains of Vermont, and they replied: "Hurlburt is telling the truth. The man he met is a highly developed master who visits earth from a star beyond Andromeda called Cessna. We do not know why the girl in question denies her part in the story, unless she was pledged by John to secrecy."

They then added that the incident could also have been blotted from her memory through a form of hypnosis at which our space brothers and sisters are apparently adept.

Readers of *Threshold to Tomorrow* will recall mention of my ebullient, red-headed friend Shirlee Teabo of Seattle, Washington, and of her spirit guide called Xan. Since then Shirlee has published a book, *Evolution of a Psychic*, in which she tells of an eerie encounter with a space being whom my Guides have since identified.

Her adventure began one Friday afternoon in 1959 while driving from Aberdeen to her home in the suburbs of Seattle. She said that she barely noticed the tall, angular man hunched at the shoulder of a curving stretch of highway, and had never before picked up a hitchhiker; yet for some reason she felt an inner compulsion to offer this one a lift. Almost without volition she backed her car along the shoulder of the freeway, but began to tremble with fright when he slid into the seat beside her.

"Don't be afraid, Shirlee," she reports that he said, and she wondered how he could have known her name. Neither the registration card behind the visor, nor her closed purse could have offered a clue. She noted other odd things about her new companion. Although it was a steaming summer day, he wore a heavy pin-striped suit with wide out-of-date lapels, and a wide-brimmed black hat pulled low over his eyes. Suddenly he was telling her things about herself that she had never told anyone, and she had the weird sensation that she had known him all her life.

Increasingly suspicious, she pulled into a roadside restaurant area, hoping that the hitchhiker would look for another ride. But he followed her inside, and sat quietly while she ordered coffee and an ice-cream cone, declining anything for himself. She decided that he probably had no money; so when her order arrived she impulsively handed him the cone. "He studied it a long time, before cautiously taking a lick," she recalls. "A delighted smile spread across his face as he attacked the ice cream voraciously. It was obvious that this guy had never seen ice cream before."

They returned to the car, and were cruising through Tacoma before Shirlee realized that she had no idea of her passenger's destination. "Oh, this'll be fine," he said vaguely. She stopped the car, and as he climbed out Shirlee surprised herself by handing him a ten dollar bill, saying, "Don't think of returning it. If you ever meet someone who needs it, just pass it along."

"He smiled then, and called good-bye," she continued, "and as I pulled back onto the roadway I glanced in the rearview mirror for a last glimpse of my gangling friend. He was gone. I pulled off the road, looking frantically up and down the highway. There was nowhere for him to hide, yet he was nowhere to be seen. He had vanished. If he had existed at all! I rummaged quickly through my purse, confirming that it was definitely ten dollars lighter.''

On reaching home, she said, ''My family was on the verge of committing me to a padded room, as I raved on about the man who had all but disappeared before my very eyes. 'It's probably the heat,' my sister-in-law Edna suggested. No one believed me.''

At her mother's insistence Shirlee retired to her bedroom to lie down, and Edna went home to prepare dinner for her husband; but she stopped to talk to some neighbors along the way. An hour later Edna telephoned, and in a strained voice demanded that Shirlee come over right away. Still irritated that her sister-in-law doubted her story, Shirlee refused; but Edna, sounding almost hysterical, said ''You must'' and rang off. Alarmed that something might have happened to one of the children, Shirlee rushed to her brother's house and found Edna drinking coffee with a neighbor known to her only as Everett.

''He was as pale as the ash of the cigarette he raised to his lips with trembling hands,'' Shirlee recounted. ''Everett traveled for a tire company and had just returned from a sales trip to eastern Washington. He had been driving through the desert near Ephrata when he saw a man standing along the side of the road. The country there is dry, hot and flat, so flat that you can see for miles in any direction. Since there wasn't much traffic on the highway, Everett had stopped to give the man a lift."

Everett said that the hitchhiker was wearing a dark pin-striped suit, with a black hat pulled down over his eyes, "and he must have sensed how uneasy I was because he said, 'Don't be afraid, Everett.' That man knew my name before I even said a word! That just scared me more."

He had driven no more than a mile when the stranger suddenly asked to be let out. "Are you sure you want out here?" Everett protested, as he pulled to the side of the highway. After all, there was no sign of habitation nearby. The man said that would be fine, and as he walked toward the back of the car, Everett wondered if he was doing the right thing, to leave him in such a forsaken stretch of country.

"At first I was going to drive on," Everett told Shirlee, "but it was just too hot to leave him stranded out there." Everett turned to urge that the stranger get back in the car, but he had vanished. And there was no place for him to hide.

When the badly shaken salesman reached home, his wife was agog with Shirlee's strange tale that she had heard from Edna only a short time before. The combined families pondered the mystery through two pots of coffee, but could arrive at no explanation. As Shirlee phrased the question: How could anyone be at two different places separated by a hundred miles at approximately the same time?

As is invariably the case, an encounter with a space person does not leave the earthling untouched. Soon Shirlee found that she was talking in her dreams with a being called Xan, whom she recognized as her hitchhiking friend although he was now wearing a white robe. As time went by, she began receiving telepathic messages from him during a meditative state, and her psychic abilities matured so rapidly that she is now a widely accepted psychic counselor.

The Guides say of her original encounter: "The man was indeed Xan, who was manifesting to help her more speedily develop her innate psychic talents. He sent proof to her by appearing at nearly the same time to the man in the desert. These are real manifestations of the ability of space people to appear and disappear by rearranging the atoms. Xan is a space person from the Andromeda galaxy, but he also knew Shirlee in a previous earthly life in ancient Persia."

CHAPTER SIX

Planetary Travels

AN outstanding example of the type of space being who was born into an earthly body is a seventy-five-year-old part Cherokee Indian who also descends from European nobility and from the renowned American patriot, Patrick Henry. An artist, sculptor, educator, costume designer and philosopher, William Goodlett has made a dozen out-of-body visits to other planets from his stately old Victorian house in Salem, Virginia.

My introduction to him came through a cassette tape that he mailed to me after reading *Threshold to Tomorrow*. Ordinarily I do not play the tapes with which I am inundated by some readers who apparently find it easier to communicate by voice than by writing. To me it is a time-consuming chore, since I can read and reply to a letter in minutes, but must devote an entire afternoon to hearing only a few tapes, after assembling my equipment. But some inner compulsion prompted me to play this particular tape the day that it arrived, and I was so captivated by the sender's account of his out-of-body visitations that I asked the Guides about him at our next day's session.

"The man from Salem," they began, "is an astonishing extraterrestrial himself, in that he visits many planets, has total recall, and yet is at home on the planet earth where he chooses to spend most of this lifetime, having been born into a gifted tribe that had previously come from another planet when the earth was being restructured after a shift on its axis some 23,000 years ago. Some of his space travels are to the planet where he once lived, and others are new and exciting to him."

The following day the Guides elaborated further on William Goodlett, writing: "He is of particular interest as a type of space being who deliberately chose to come here from another galaxy to understand earth life and to help earthlings realize that we are all one. A very good man indeed. He was born into that body, choosing a Cherokee heritage because that tribe began in his own native planet, which he has visited while in spirit form. It is in the Orion constellation."

Intrigued, I telephoned Mr. Goodlett to tell him what the Guides had said, and when my husband and I later drove to Salem, Virginia, to interview him we learned a great deal more about one of the most fascinating men that I have ever known. Widely traveled throughout the world, he was in the South Pacific with the U.S. Army Medical Corps when World War II ended, had written a book on post-operative physical exercises for the

Second Army, and served as a cryptographer dealing in weather codes during the war. Thanks to the expertise gained in that latter work, he has codified the English language in order to teach reading phonetically, and now tutors both adults and children in this system. A heart attack in 1966 ended his work as a dancing master and costume designer, but with the aid of a pacemaker he is now able to teach art at four weekly classes, instruct Boy Scouts and other lads in Indian dances and chants, and teach the reading classes.

His mother, Mabel Helen Hesse, founded and conducted a school in Roanoke that was structured on the methods of Maria Montessori. Her mother, Clara Belle Henry, was a great-great-granddaughter of Patrick Henry through a double connection (cousins who married); and on her father's side Mabel Helen was a direct descendant of Frederick II of Hesse. The Hesse monarchy sold 27,000 soldiers to George III of England for three million dollars, to fight against the American colonies during the Revolutionary War; and afterwards, since neither Hesse nor England wanted them back, the surviving mercenaries settled throughout Ohio and Pennsylvania, becoming U.S. citizens.

William Goodlett's father, Earl Gordon Goodlett, was a well-known geologist, who opened numerous pyrite mines in Alabama and Virginia. He was a great-grandson of Red Feather, a Cherokee Indian in Tennessee, and his Goodlett grandfather was a Presbyterian minister who founded numerous churches, and for whom the town of Goodlettsville, Tennessee, was named.

Earl evinced no interest whatsoever in his Indian heritage. It remained for the son, William, to help carry on the traditions of the Cherokees, to whom he is known as the "Medicine Man of Virginia" because of his proven powers to bring rain, or to stop rainstorms that are not wanted. For thirty-five years he has been Indian lore counselor for the Boy Scouts of his area, and has taught them a Cherokee chant that for some mysterious reason seems to bring them apported objects or coins when most needed.

In two instances of extreme crises, once with barrage balloons during World War II in San Francisco, and the other while leading Boy Scouts on a camping maneuver, Goodlett instantly teleported himself to the scene to rescue others. He cannot explain the phenomenon, but he has numerous witnesses to both events.

The Guides say of this extraordinary man: "This is not his first earthly incarnation, but he had been in the Orion galaxy for a long time by earthly accounting. He naturally feels nostalgia for that native galaxy, yet he came to earth to help others advance. The Cherokees occupied a planet in the Orion constellation for millennia until some of them agreed to inhabit the reburgeoning earth after the last shift on its axis. They settled in Atlantis, and when that continent sank some twelve thousand years ago they knew by advance knowledge to move westward in time to rehabilitate themselves on the eastern part of what became North America. They were always able to retain remnants of their once great civilization in Atlantis, despite the loss of most technological know-how, and were a grand race whose phenomenal memories served them well in preserving their folklore. Since they were from a hogan planet where Goodlett also resided, and he had originally come to earth with that segment of his people for one lifetime, he felt more at home in this lifetime to find good parents in that area, and to share his father's Cherokee blood.''

William Goodlett had the first of his other-world experiences on February 18, 1968, two years after the heart attack that thereafter limited his active physical endeavors. As he has done after each subsequent experience, he immediately wrote down all that he had seen, and he says of these strange occurrences: "They are not dreams, because in a dream I seem to be watching myself from outside, but in these experiences I am in my body with all of my senses—sight, smell, taste, touch and hearing—or am in the bodies of other beings. One time I was actually a ball of light. At first I could not understand what was happening, until I recently began reading books by people who had had somewhat similar space travels, and I realized that I'd been having out-of-body experiences.''

Of that first encounter, he says: "I'm standing in front of a small hill of dark-colored rocks. The area is cold—not a penetrating, but a thin, unmoving cold of which I seem to be a part. I'm looking at the sun. It's less than half the size as seen from earth, and is fainter, so that it can be looked at directly. It is near the horizon of the rocky plain in front of me. I am not a human of earthly origin. My body is small, about four feet high, and very thin. My arms are longer than an earthling's, as are my fingers. I do not seem to have on many clothes, just some straps, but I wear a fedora-type hat with a wide brim, and buskin-type shoes that reach halfway to my knees. I have thick, dark olive-green skin and my eyes seem to be larger than a human's. The earth shines in the heavens to my right, and Jupiter is a brilliant glow to my left. I do not

move, but simply stand and look at earth and the
sun. Then I wonder what the earth man to whom I
have flashed the sight that I am seeing thinks, and
I awaken from the trance.''

Oh, dear! Shades of little green men from Mars!
I almost turned off the cassette, but something
prompted me to persist, and Goodlett's voice continued: ''Four years later, on May 7, 1972, I had
another experience. There were three of us. I was
quite old and thin, but not feeble. About seven feet
tall. I had a long beard and long gray hair, and was
dressed in a heavy, belted robe. Over this I wore a
shawl or cape with long fringe, and I carried a tall
staff. With me was a young girl of about eighteen,
with clear complexion and long, wavy dark hair,
dressed in a long frock embroidered with bands of
color around the neckline, hem, and edges of the
long, loose sleeves. We were accompanied by a
young man who was heavily built, with wide shoulders and long wavy hair, who was clad in a knee-
length dress with wide borders of embroidery, dark
brown in color, with blue and yellow accents.''

At this point I should mention that Goodlett,
being an artist, was able after each of his planetary
visits to paint in watercolor the people and settings
that he encountered, and they make for fascinating
study. And now to continue his recollection:

''We were walking down a trail of sandy gravel
about twenty feet wide, through a forest of what
seemed like oak trees, except that each of them
was two or three times bigger around than the
giant sequoias that I have seen out west. They
were spaced quite far apart and seemed to reach
several hundred feet in the air. The trail led between two hills, and on the left one was a large
barn, several outbuildings, and a large house with

sagging roof and walls fallen into decay, although the barn seemed to be in good condition. There was no underbrush in the forest, just brown dried grasses, and near the house was a light on a tall post that flickered like a gaslight. We seemed to be in a rush to reach a highway, and the girl turned to me saying, 'Hurry, Grandpa, we'll be late.' She smiled and took my hand, and we hurried down the trail to reach the road that appeared to be paved with loose crushed slate.

"Coming up the hill from the left were several huge wagons whose wheels were ten feet high and made of solid wood. They were pulled by animals as large as elephants that looked like pigs with dog faces. There were six or eight in the teams pulling the wagons, and they seemed to be enjoying the work. One of them turned around and looked like he would laugh out loud at the animal behind him, although I don't remember hearing a sound. Then, as we stood watching by the road, the experience faded away. It was an overcast day, but not dark, and the area smelled like lemons. I remember feeling amazed at the size of the wagons, although the huge animals seemed familiar; and at sight of the crumbling houses there was a feeling of sadness, as if it were a part of my past that the young people with me could not enjoy. It seemed that a catastrophe had occurred to destroy many people and places, and that the young people and I had trudged many miles through the forest just to see the wagons pass by."

I asked the Guides if they could identify this sad-sounding planet, and they said that it was in a "location near to the Dog Star." Consulting the dictionary, I learned that the latter is properly called Sirius, in Canis Major, so the planet visited by

Goodlett is apparently a nearby but lesser member of that galaxy. The Guides said that it had suffered "an invasion from other planetary beings, and Goodlett indeed remembered it from a previous lifetime there long ago."

Another four years passed before Goodlett apparently visited another planet, and a strange one indeed. He said that in March of 1976 he found himself on a planet whose air was liquid, although it was inhabited by beings similar to humans, with two arms and two legs, thick skin of a creamy color, fingers, hands, large eyes, and long hair that seemed to be floating in the liquid air. They were no more than four feet tall, and progress was made by walking rather than swimming, as the air seemed to be of a very thin fluid.

"They had one long street that wound back and forth along the side of a huge cliff similar to the walls of the Grand Canyon," he recalled. "The houses were five or six to a row on different levels, dug into the sides of the wall, and were all lighted with a soft, phosphorescent glow. I walked where the others did, and attracted notice because of my height, although they seemed accustomed to creatures other than themselves. They wore a short dresslike garment of a silky texture that floated around them in the liquid atmosphere, and although none of them spoke to me, they smiled with a huge grin across the bottom of their faces.

"I followed the upward path, going from one short street to another for a long distance, and the light became brighter as I approached the surface. Others were going with me to the outside atmosphere which was very thin, but so charged with oxygen that we felt exhilarated. It was also liquid, but of a thinner variety, and there was a seashore on which the inhabitants were sitting while children leaped through the air, playing leapfrog and turning a couple of somersaults before landing in front of the next child. The sun was not visible, as the sky was heavily overcast with a layer of thick, brilliant clouds hanging so low that you could almost reach up and touch them, and they kept moving back and forth in large billows. I was curious about the surface of the seashore, and on stooping down to examine it saw that it was similar to the sand at Daytona Beach—soft, wet and very firm.''

Oddly enough, four years had elapsed between each of those first three out-of-body experiences, but only one month later a fourth one occurred that excited Goodlett so greatly that he yearns for an opportunity to return to the place of this sojourn. He recounts that on the evening of April 13, 1976, he found himself walking along a city street in a residential section without trees, but with plots of grass. It was night, but the scene was brightly lighted by several moons in the heavens.

''No one was about,'' he continued. ''The houses were of wood, with many small windows that had inside shutters—all closed so that brightly painted geometrical designs or flowers showed from the outside. I seemed to be in a great hurry, but realized that I was not quite materialized. It must be like a ghost feels, because I could see through myself. When I reached a certain house I hastened up a short walk to a sort of entryway and started to knock at the door, which was immediately opened by an extremely tall, dark gray being who was shaped like a human, but had no nose. Two holes in his face were nostrils, and he had large, bushy eyebrows over small eyes. He was dressed in a short tunic that was decorated with many jeweled medallions. He reached out and took my hand, saying, 'Come in, will you? We were expecting you.' Well, gosh, I certainly was surprised at that, but as I took his hand and stepped over the doorstep I instantly materialized. I was in my body exactly as I am now. I entered the house, which seemed to be only one very large room, and saw a long row of very weird beings, all different, and I understood without being told that they were from different planets and were holding a conference. There was no furniture, and they were all sitting on the floor on both sides of the long room.

"One of them who was taller than I, but seemed more like me than the others, came and stood by me and 'thought' to me. He didn't say a word but I could hear what he was thinking. Several of the others then came up to welcome me, and most of them clapped, for they had hands. One was about five feet tall, with a large bulbous head and no neck. He had a large wide mouth, large ears, long body, short legs, and a crest, instead of hair, that ran crosswise from one ear to the other. He rippled as he walked, as if he had no bones or frame, and there was a protuberance like a small kangaroo pouch on his front. He came up to me, grinned broadly, clasped his two hands and bowed. The being next to me said that he was welcoming me with that gesture, and that I should do likewise, so I clasped my hands and bowed. Another being that seemed to be all head like an octopus, except for four short legs and feet, bent over and touched me with the top of his head. I felt no alarm, because they all seemed to know that I was there in spirit and were trying to help me stay long enough to communicate.

"Each being was different, and one whom I understood to be a female went over to another tiny being to greet him. Her body was very like a chicken's, except that she was about four feet tall, and while I watched she suddenly expanded her backside like a huge rose in the face of the little round one. My communicator explained that she was giving off her delicate and lovely scent to welcome the other being. I remember how surprised I felt at that! Many of the creatures had shapes more related to earth people, and most were dark in color, some with leathery skin, although a couple of them were fair. I enquired and was told that most suns were so hot that dark, thick skins were a protection, and that on the planet I was visiting no one went outside when the sun was shining. They spent the days inside resting or working, and undertook their outdoor activities at night, by the light of the several moons.''

Goodlett said that at this point he began to fade away, and the communicator grabbed him by the shoulders, saying, "Oh, don't go! Stay! We want to talk to you." A being about two feet high, covered with what seemed to be orange fur, ran over and grabbed his legs tightly, pleading, "Oh, don't go, don't go, don't go." And although he felt himself making a real effort to remain, his own body dissolved and he awakened from the experience. Then he immediately wrote down all of his recollections, and painted pictures of the various beings that he had seen. He feels that an assemblage of interplanetary beings was in progress, and that they were exceptionally pleased to have a representative from planet earth. He keeps hoping to attend another one, and next time to hear the discussions.

Goodlett recalls that on his next extraterrestrial

visit some twenty-eight months later, he discovered that he was a woman of about twenty, with long dark hair, wearing a long brown dress of heavy homespun material. He was lying on his back on a dirt bank, his feet hanging over the edge and contemplating the stars in the night sky. His/her mother was working in a nearby vegetable garden, because they could not go out in the daylight sun. To the right was a doorway in a small mound of earth leading to their underground home, and to the left on a high hill was a large domed satellite with yellow light shining from its many windows, through which he could see a robot testing an organ that it had just constructed for them.

Suddenly two girls came galloping into view on horses twice the size of earthly ones, although the girls were "normal" size. One leaned down and asked something of the robot, who came out of the satellite and pointed to Goodlett (the young woman) and the mother. Goodlett says of this strange occurrence: "The girls did not speak, but the thoughts of the horses came to us: 'Are you real? Are you people?' "

He said that the females slid off the horses and embraced him and his mother, saying, "Oh, we're so glad. One of the horses saw a light and told us. We have ridden eight hours to get here. The messenger came to us yesterday. We didn't know you were here." His/her father, who had a white beard, and the robot then joined the group and they entered the tunnel to their underground house, while the horses gazed through the doorway.

"We all seemed wonderfully happy to find more humans," Goodlett added, "and I seemed to know that some catastrophe had occurred to destroy human life, but that people were beginning to return to the planet. It could not have been a future glimpse of planet earth, however, because the stars were placed so differently in the heavens, and some were so close together that they resembled suns. It was nothing like our sky.''

Goodlett feels that he may actually have pinpointed the location of only one of the planets that he has seemingly visited while out of his body. This occurred on June 15, 1980, when he found himself riding down a swift-flowing river in a bargelike boat that was open at the top and had a row of ten seats. He was talking to the driver, who sat at a wheel in front and who told him that the entire planet was dotted with small islands. There were no continents, and the horizon seemed so close that the water looked to be flowing over the edge.

''The driver seemed to know that I was a visitor to the planet,'' he said, ''and I had a feeling that other-planetary visitors came there rather frequently. We left the boat at a dock on an island, and I went with a young man up a path to some buildings, and on the roof of one of them we leaned over a parapet to look out at the land, which was seemingly all farms and trees. The island looked to be about five miles across, with the horizon quite close and ocean surrounding it on all sides. A small red sun was just going down, but smaller suns about a tenth the size of our full moons still cast a twilight as the stars began to come out. I saw in the heavens a square formation of brilliant stars and remarked that it looked something like our Little Dipper. The young man responded, 'It is, except you're on the other side of it and much nearer.' Well, golly, I realized that he must have been on earth at some time if he knew what it looked like on the other side. Its formation was about fifteen degrees above the horizon in the west, and about twenty degrees to the right of the sunset was a bright band of stars crossing the sky, like the Milky Way but much more brilliant. Individual blue, red, yellow and green stars twinkled among lots of white ones, with some heat projecting from that area. I asked the young man about that, and he said, 'Yes, the climate is always the same here. It's not like you have it at all.' It was so obvious that he had been on earth and knew about our conditions here, that I awakened in astonishment. Then, by studying books on astronomy I found that on the other side of the Little Dipper from us, in the constellation Cepheus, is a brilliant red star called the Garnet star, and I am just about convinced that it is the 'sun' around which the little planet that I visited revolves.''

One of Goodlett's more curious sensations occurred March 25, 1981, when he discovered himself to be a ball of light conversing with a similar being as they floated through the air. "I was a pale blue ball about the size of a basketball,'' he said, "and the other one was somewhat larger, a pale yellow color with a slight tinge of red glowing in the center. We were about a hundred feet above ground that was covered with clumps of blue grass and blue bushes. Groups of from ten to thirty brown animals of several species were grazing, and the largest were the size of horses, but thinner, with longer necks and long hair. As we watched, some of these creatures formed a circle facing the center and began a sad song, 'Where are our beautiful two-legs? Why have they gone away? Oh, where are our beautiful two-legs? Oh sad, unlucky day.' And they wept tears and leaned their heads and long necks on one another. Some of the colts asked what the two-legs had been like, and the horses raised up on their hind legs saying, 'They walked like this. When you're older you can go someday to the large hills and there's one made of stone that you can see, but it's not beautiful like ours were.' There were several clusters of two-story wooden houses, but the windows and doors were boarded up, and I wondered at the time where the wood had been obtained, since I saw no trees.

"The being who floated alongside me remarked, 'Our two-legs all died. A fungus ate them up, and they closed their houses.' I asked what they were like, and he said, 'They were like yours except all blue, and some had yellow and some brown hair. They used to play games with the four-legs. Do you have any that would like to live here?' I told him that in some of our islands in tropical seas there were brown people who had become immune to fungus diseases, and perhaps he could persuade them to visit the planet to see if they'd like to stay. I also remarked that there was a legend that in the long-ago past we had some people who were also pale blue. He said, 'Is that what you call them, people? We called them two-legs.' The animals took no notice of us, and I wondered if a similar fungus could have destroyed some of our prehistoric societies whose artifacts are now covered by jungles or sand. I have no idea where in the galaxy that planet is located."

Goodlett said he was struck by the fact that he observed no directional shadows, and being an artist he would have noticed that. He saw no sun, but the light was all pervasive.

In mid-afternoon of February 19, 1982, Goodlett lay down on a couch and was just beginning to doze, when he found himself in two places at once.

He could feel the couch beneath him and the clothes
on his body, but simultaneously he was a midget
about three feet high riding with three other tiny
beings, in one of a series of little open cars being
pulled by a single engine up a mountainside covered with beautiful gardens of flowers and trees.

"The little train was running on a track with
many horseshoe turns, or switchbacks," he recalls, "which carried us first on one side of the
mountain and then back on a higher level, so that
we could see about fifty feet below us and for
miles into the distance where there were other
peaks like ours. Some of the flowers that we passed
were as large as the rooms in our earth houses, in
astonishingly beautiful colors. I could feel a tremendous strength of body and muscle, as if I could
lift the car in which we were riding, and our bodies
seemed to be much more dense than earth bodies.
We all had dark brown skin, and bushy, straight
black hair, large round heads, large eyes, and bulg-
ing, muscular arms and legs. Our shirts and pants
were quite tight fitting, but comfortable like a double knit, and very colorful. The sky was completely overcast, but cloudless, and the light seemed
quite bright. I subconsciously knew that this planet
was much larger than earth. My companions seemed
to know that I was sending back impressions to the
earth body on the couch, and would keep pointing
out things for me to tell him."

Goodlett recalls in bafflement that as the train
was slowly climbing the mountain peak, a midget
about three cars behind his jumped out and ran
through the garden to where a little being about ten
inches long, with a human-shaped body but the
long wings of a dragonfly, was hovering over the
exotic flowers. The midget grabbed the tiny being,

saying, "Oh, look; I got one, I got one," whereupon the fairy, or child-fly bit him on the wrist, and the midget disappeared. The others looked at each other, saying, "He shouldn't have done that; he shouldn't have done that."

And that incident, Goodlett remarks, is the only time that he ever witnessed anything approaching violence on any of the planets.

The four out-of-body experiences of William Goodlett that I consider most significant are repeat visits to two different planets, one of which the Guides say is his native environment. That is the "hogan" planet, and I will save it until last, although several other visitations interrupted the sequence.

One of his visits, and perhaps the most fantastic, occurred on June 18, 1982, when he "asked" to go to another planet before lying down at 7 P.M. Suddenly he found himself in the body of a birdman, who was about seven feet tall, with a thin body, long thin legs, and six-feet-long wings where his shoulders would have been. Below the wings were long, thin arms with hands attached, and except for those and his legs he was covered with feathers from the neck down. His head was human.

"I was on a hillside with many dense trees, where a small patch of cleared ground was being planted with bulbs by normal-sized humans under my supervision," he recounted. "I was showing them how to separate the clumps of bulbs and plant them a foot apart. The bulbs were about the size of small onions, and we were expecting them to grow as large as pumpkins. The humans seemed to be new colonists on the planet and were being taught by my race how to grow edible plants. My mother, a birdwoman, was with me and said telepathically, 'They learned this quickly, but we must feed them until the crops will grow.' I asked if she thought the colonists would be any danger to us, and she said, 'No, they can't be a danger because our ways of life are too different. But we can be a help to each other.' She turned then and walked up a small road leading to another clearing in the trees at the top of the hill, and I continued to show the men how to use a small trowel to place the bulbs. As it began to get darker I told them that it was a long way through the trees to their cave, and I also had a long way to go, but would meet them there the next day. Then I ran lightly up the little road, seemingly not weighing much, as I bounced easily up the steep hill much as a robin would run, with quick little steps. From the top of the hill I could see that the other side was rocky, with bare trees, and below stretched a rocky desert plain. The hill dropped sharply like a cliff, and I folded my arms over the lower part of my chest, which bulged with huge muscles from the shoulder area down to the center of my body, spread out my folded wings and began to beat them with powerful strokes. I could feel the effort while doing it, and began making rapid speed as I soared upward on a draft of air. The sun was a deep rosy red behind a veil of thin clouds, and I sailed toward the sunset. Then I saw my dwelling place where we birdmen lived—rude shelters with many open rooms in rows, somewhat like open garages, under one roof.

"In each of the large rooms were piles of grasses like huge nests, where we seemed to squat to rest and sleep. I observed nothing resembling a kitchen or dining room, but in some of the rooms were huge books, as big as a spread-out newspaper and almost a foot thick, on shelves in the rear. This showed signs of intellect, and I seemed to realize that our race was much older than mankind, and vastly more intelligent. Our chief pleasure was in the invention of machines for other races to use. For food we caught a kind of lizard and small animals like rabbits by dropping nets on them, and we picked and ate many fruits and raw vegetables. We did not cook. I sailed down to a landing in front of one of the rooms, or nests, and then I woke up here.''

Goodlett says that he was so excited by the experience that every night he kept saying, "Oh, I want to go back. I want to visit there again. Take me back," and one week later his wish was granted. This time, however, he was not in the body of a birdman, but in his human form, although he was sailing through the air beside a birdman, "who was on my left, slightly higher, with his outstretched wings over me. I was simply moving along with my arms folded over my chest, and every now and then he'd give a gentle beat of his wings and glide slightly above me.

"I asked him his name, and he said, 'We have no names. We are all one. We can talk to each other any time. The books you saw are antiques. We do not use them, as our knowledge is all memorized and always available to each of us.' Well, that answer let me know that he knew I had been in his body on the previous experience, for how else would he know that I had seen the books? I asked his age, and he replied, 'I do not know in your time. I came here with others long, long ago from a dying world. We chose this one because it is near the center of the galaxy and always warm. The density is nearly like that of your world, but it is smaller. Our other home was larger and less dense, out on the edge of the galaxy. We do not age anymore.' Well, that answer told me that he had been here, because he knew so much about the earth.''

Goodlett said that they settled to the ground before a large, beautiful building with a blue roof and outer walls paved in mosaics. Inside were huge and auditoriumlike rooms with approximately forty-foot ceilings, no windows, and no discernible lights, although they were brilliantly lit. ''There were large worktables like those in an architect's office,'' he said, ''and over on the side many single machines of odd shapes and sizes. Working there were a few humans, but also some twenty different kinds of beings like those I had seen at the planetary convention—the one I so want to return to. I asked the birdman what the various beings were doing, and his answer was, 'They are going to school, learning how to do many complex things, just like you're doing on earth. You're going to school now, and have been for many lifetimes.' Boy! That answer just sort of bowled me over. We walked into the next room and over to a big table there, and he said, 'Let me show you this.' He picked up a small metal box about five inches square and two inches deep, saying, 'This is a robot brain that will run an automatic ship. It is the latest thing I have made. The ship is very large and will load itself, sail for another port and unload itself. If the weather is bad it will sink under the surface and keep going until the weather improves. It will be used on many planets where there are oceans, but not here.' I asked what their spaceships look like and he answered, 'We do not need any. We simply go instantly to our destination, taking what we need.'

I asked if he'd been to earth, and he said, 'Oh yes, many times, but we do not appear there like this.' ''

Goodlett said he realized at the time that if the birdmen changed their appearance while visiting earth, they undoubtedly looked like humans, and that we had probably talked to them without knowing it. While he was musing about this, the birdman asked, "Do you remember the robot that made an organ for you to play?" Astonished, Goodlett replied, "Yes, but then I was a young girl" [in that earlier visit to a different planet]. The birdman responded, "I made the robot for you. We send them many places where they can help."

"Well, that gave me quite a puzzle to think about," Goodlett declared. "He knew that I had been on the planet where the robot was, but was that in my past, was it coincident with the present life I'm now living, or is it in the future? Or is time meaningless because the planets are in different parts of the galaxies? There were many more questions I wanted to ask the birdman, but suddenly I was back in my own body at 3 A.M., remembering the flight through the air and how my hair ruffled in the breeze, the appearance of the birdman, and of the beings who were not humans. Some were short and thick bodied, others seven or eight feet tall and spidery looking, with four arms and an antenna. Some wore long cloaks and resembled monks, while only the birdpeople had wings. I had the impression that the latter regarded the rest of us as little children and themselves as patient teachers."

These two encounters sounded so extraordinary that I again asked the Guides about William Goodlett, and they replied: "He has indeed made those travels and has appeared on other planets. So have

many others, and his attendance at the galactic
conference will soon be repeated in more detail.
As for the birdman experience, there are many
planets where the souls appear in different bodies
that are acclimated to the conditions there, and he
was indeed in a bird body on his first trip, in spirit
of course, and in his present body the second time.
In the future there will be earthlings inhabiting
other planets and traveling there by teleportation,
as he does now, for the earth will become a rather
inhospitable planet for a time after the shift on its
axis, and many other planets will welcome the
arrival of earthlings.''

If this is all true, and the Guides insist that it is,
then Goodlett's warm welcome on various planets
should remove our fear of strange environments
and the question of our personal survival after the
earth shifts on its axis at the end of this century.

And now we come to the two visits that Goodlett
paid to the planet that the Guides have identified
as his native realm. In the first, which occurred
February 7, 1982, he was a man in his early thirties
weighing about 150 pounds, five feet five inches
tall, with long brown hair and a beard.

''There's an older man sitting next to me,'' he
recalls, ''dressed in a long skin cloak, with gray
hair and a long gray beard. We are in my house, a
large, circular room about thirty or forty feet in
diameter. The walls are upright logs or poles touching each other, and sunk into the ground. A roof of
logs or beams is overhead. There is an opening in
one side covered by a cloth drape. We are sitting
on large flat stones at the end of a circular depres-
sion about eighteen inches deep and five or six feet
across. The bottom is covered with sand, and in
the middle of it is a stone fireplace with a small fire

burning. The smoke and heat are rising toward an open hole in the roof.''

Switching to past tense, Goodlett continued his narrative, saying: ''It was something like the Navajo hogans I have seen out west, but we were not Indians, we were Caucasians. I also knew that we had a mild, cool climate. The older man was telling me that the Chief would give me a thousand, or perhaps as high as three thousand measures of grain for my eldest daughter, who was about fifteen years old, to become his son's wife. I was aware that the Chief had several sons, and that I had ten children and two wives. The boy was to become part of the bride's family and work for me. This would be his dowry, and I was planning to go to another part of the land and open up a new section to farm. We were all farmers, but settled a long distance from each other in a land of low, rolling hills with some lakes and streams. I did not see this, but simply knew it as we discussed the dowry, in another language whose meaning I was automatically translating into English while I was in the body of this man.

''I did not see the boy, but knew that he was a slender young man, blond and long-haired, named David. We were dressed in knee-length cloaks belted at the waist. Our pants were tied from the ankles up by crossed straps to the knees, and we wore heavy skin boots that reached slightly higher than the ankles. We sat with our feet down in the pit, resting them on the sandy bottom in front of the fire. The old man was going to see the Chief and try to get a good bargain for me, for the boy. There was no one else in the house with us at the time, but I could hear talking outside. I felt very comfortable and at home there.''

Seventeen months elapsed between his two visits to the hogan planet, and as remarked earlier, several trips to other planets intervened. Meanwhile he had suffered another heart attack and was now wearing a pacemaker. Just before dropping off to sleep on July 24, 1983, he fervently asked to visit another planet, "and slowly, through a mist, the scene appeared before me and I was suddenly there, seated in a low chair with high back. Two feet in front of me was a little low table with a cloth on it, along with two large wooden bowls, one containing mixed vegetables and the other small pieces of what tasted like yak meat. I was eating. So were about twenty other people, seated cross-legged on the floor at individual low tables in a circle around the room, which had a central fireplace pit like the other one, but this was not the same hogan I had sat in before."

Goodlett said that several months before this visitation he had taken erythromycin for a bronchial infection, and the medicine had destroyed his smell and taste buds. "But while I was sitting there eating, in this other body, it suddenly dawned on me that I was tasting the yak meat and I thought, Oh good, my taste has come back!

"I was on the right of the doorway, and there were two other older men, and a boy. The rest were women and girls. We each had our own bowls of vegetables and meat, and we ate with wooden spoons about three times the size of our tablespoons. I saw no knives or forks, but some of the bowls had beautiful carved designs on them, and all of the tables had cloth covers. Several women were coming and going through the doorway, serving the food that they brought in from the outside. I saw no drinking cups or glasses. We were all talking and laughing together in a language not English, but which I could readily understand. We were short, stocky people with fair skin and brown hair. On finishing the meal, one of the men shook hands with me, using both hands to say good-bye. I grabbed his right hand, as we do here when we shake hands; then he put his left hand on top of our clasped hands and I put my left hand on top of his, and we shook all four hands together.

"Afterwards we all went outside, and saw about fifty women and girls standing among a large group of pony-dogs that were individually hitched to sleds with high sides. The pony-dogs, because that is what we called them in that other language, were about the size of miniature Shetland ponies, but they had split hooves like deer, and their heads were rather doglike, with long hair and drooping ears. The sleds were shaped something like an old-fashioned bathtub, but smaller, and their high curved runners were wide, like skis. There was a kind of double harness on the animals, circled around the neck and lower around the chest behind their front legs. Each woman and girl had a long staff with streamers about two feet long and small tassels on the end, which they waved in front of the pony-dogs to start them off.

"I was holding a long staff with blue streamers and leading the journey with one of the other men. We went slowly over the land, which was thickly covered with grasses from one to two feet high, over which the loaded sleds passed easily. There were as many ponies and sleds as there were people, and we did not move in a line, but were spread out as much as three city blocks apart. The sleds were piled high with bundles wrapped in cloth and tied, but were apparently light in weight, because the pony-dogs pulled them with little effort. We went over small rolling hills much like those in Missouri, and in some of the valleys were small spring branches, but shallow, and I saw no soil erosion. After a seemingly all-day trip I was tired when we came to a cluster of hogans, some in valleys and some in the hills, but all empty. During the journey the sky was mostly overcast, but a gentle wind blew and the cool air smelled like lemons, as it did on that other planet that I've already told about.

"Through occasional breaks in the clouds we could see above us another planet about three times as large as our moon, very green looking, and we could even see the clouds on it, too. This seemed to be an overnight rest stop, and we began partly to unload the sleds and unhitch the pony-dogs, who started to run and play like puppies, and eat the grasses. As I was carrying some bundles into the hogan that apparently was mine, a little girl who seemed about twelve years old said to me, 'Where do you go, father, when you're not with us?' I laughed and said, 'Come here, child. Now, when the clouds part, see our sister planet up there? I go to be with our other family there.' Well, the first time I had been on this hogan planet, I knew that I had two families and ten children, but I didn't realize then that one family was on a different planet. At this point I understood that we could go there instantly, by thinking and wanting to do so. That was teleportation, and I divided my time between the two planets which revolved around each other, and also around two stars, or suns. There was a double star system around which these two planets revolved, but the other stars, or suns, were farther away, so that we did not derive much heat from them.

"All of the men on our hogan planet could teleport, and there were not many of them, but lots of women. Now my son came from one of the hogans, to show me his staff which was about eight feet long, with a bunch of long streamers and tassels that were used to flutter in front of the pony-dogs to direct them which way to go. They were not struck or guided, because we did not follow a path. My son had started the journey toward the back of the caravan, but had now caught up with us, and I want to describe what he was wearing. His clothes were made by sewing together strips of material, so that the pants were two long strips from the knees up over the shoulders and down to the knees in back. Then two strips were sewn on each side from the knee up to the waist, with two short strips inside the legs to his crotch, an apron in the front and an apron in the back. He wore a wide leather belt and a little jacket made of strips sewn together, with detachable strips for sleeves, and a turbanlike cap of strips sewn in a circle, with an inserted flat top. He had high, knee-length boots, and the entire outfit was bright yellow, with brown tassels as decoration. Well, I have designed many costumes during my lifetime, and have researched the costumes of people throughout the earth, but no costume was ever like that. Seemingly these people could only weave material in narrow strips six or eight inches in width, and would then sew the strips together to make their cloth.

"I took the staff and admired it, telling my son that it was very good because since it was slender and long he could hold it a long way in front of his (and I used a word that meant) pony-dog. These

animals were very intelligent and easily understood
our language. Then, while I waved the staff, watching the streamers flutter, I awakened in my own
body and immediately came downstairs to write
what I had seen. For one thing, it was the first time
that I remember eating and tasting something while
undergoing these experiences. I have smelled the
differences in atmosphere on the various planets,
and when I touch anything I easily remember its
feel. In seeing many of the objects I knew how
they were made, as I seem to have remembered
making them myself in previous lifetimes. Thus, all
of my senses are acutely functioning during these
out-of-body experiences. Being an artist, I noticed
almost everything that I saw, which I've drawn
and painted in twenty different pictures.''

My husband and I have seen these paintings,
which are remarkable in their clarity, and we were
particularly drawn to the depiction of the octopus-
type being who was nearly all head, except for four
little legs and four short arms. When I commented
on this creature, Goodlett remarked, ''I first saw
that being on the planet where the galactic conference was taking place—the one I so greatly wish to
return to—but I saw others like it while with the
birdman on his planet. As we walked through the
workroom where a number of different types of
beings were working, one of these octopus-beings
reached out with his little arm to an instrument
that was more than halfway across the huge table.
The arm extended itself, and the tiny hand grasped
the instrument and brought it back, as the arm
retracted back into the body. It was one of the
oddest sights of all.''

I asked if Goodlett had any further comment to
make on his strange experiences, and he replied:

"I believe that in the future there will be no such thing as spaceships; that we will be able to travel from one planet to another in this galaxy, and perhaps into other galaxies also through teleportation. Certainly these beings whom I met had teleported themselves, and I'm convinced that I was teleported by wishing and repeatedly asking to visit other planets."

Since I myself have never had these marvelous experiences, I can only quote my Guides, who commented: "By willing themselves there, space beings do indeed project themselves to other planets, just as Goodlett did in his out-of-body experiences. While on those other planets he actually trod the soil, and was seen by and conversed with others, who being more advanced than earthlings, were not at all surprised at the presence of a stranger as cohabitor of their sphere. His experiences were true and real, just as sleeping and waking are real to earthlings, and he has projected himself into other habitats and galaxies because of his previous high development and awareness of how to cope with other beings. Just as he found himself in other bodies there, so are spaceships likewise reassembled in earth's atmosphere through thought projections. And just as all things on earth began with an idea, before a desk or chair could be created, so these highly developed spacelings are able to create through the assembling of atoms and the thought process."

William Goodlett is a man of obvious integrity. I defy anyone to talk with him and doubt his sincerity. He believes every word that he speaks, is highly respected in his community, and is certainly not the victim of hallucination. A more practical, down-to-earth man I have never met, and when he expresses his firm belief that he has actually visited other planets, I can but envy him those experiences. He has obviously reached a high level in his evolvement, and I am delighted that he chose to incarnate on earth at a troubled period when we certainly need help from superior beings.

If I may be permitted a whimsical comment, I will add that I don't blame him for leaving his native hogan planet to try out another environment this time around. If I had been living on that boring planet with a lot of pony-dogs, carts and other women while the men transported themselves at will to another planet, I would volunteer for an earth life, too. We seem to have more than our share of problems here, but at least they are seldom boring.

CHAPTER SEVEN

The Arcturus Connection

ARCTURUS, one of the three brightest stars of the northern hemisphere, in the constellation Boötes, lies on a direct line with the tail of the constellation Ursa Major. The *Encyclopaedia Britannica* describes it as an orange-colored giant star forty light-years from the sun.

Because I have recently met several fascinating people who are said to have come directly to earth life from that star, I asked the Guides to describe it, and they wrote: "We have lately been to Arcturus and can tell you quite a lot about the influence that it has on souls seeking advancement there. It is a leavening star, a force for good, and it is used for honing character and instilling in those who tarry there a desire to return to their respective planets and tell everyone what they have discovered: that each of us is something of God, and that we are all one. Together we form God, and it is therefore essential that we help each other, so that all may advance together." They then identified for me a group of souls who returned to earth bodies through the natural birth process, plus their leader, who they said came back to earth from Arcturus as a Walk-in six years ago.

I first learned of this group of Arcturians in the spring of 1984 when a man named John Andreadis wrote to me from New York City, saying: "I have been familiar with your work only since last summer, when I became aware that the message in your books is identical to what I have realized through my studies of the Hindu cycles of creation. As we know, the ancient religion of India, the Sanatan Dharma, is an explanation of the eternal immutable laws of the universe, so as we understand these laws the message is always the same."

To be perfectly candid, I had never heard of the Sanatan Dharma. All that I do is transmit the Guides' messages to my readers, although I have long believed that any of us who are legitimately tapping into a fourth-dimensional source of enlightenment will receive essentially the same truths, since the fountainhead is universal wisdom.

John's letter continued: "I was reared in a very wealthy family without any religious training or guidance. However, from my earliest days religion was my deepest interest, and I began reading the Bible from the age of six. Out of the blue, at age eleven, I began practicing yoga. I sold my stereo to buy a harmonium, and would practice yoga and chant to God for three to six hours every night. At age fourteen I met my teacher, Frederick Von

Mierers, with whom I have since been studying and working, and I also studied Sanskrit and physics at Columbia University and NYU. My teacher, Frederick, is an internationally renowned Hindu astrologer and lecturer in the underlying unity between science and religion. The astrological work that he does is entirely spiritual in that its purpose is to make one conscious of the karmic entanglements that have been created through our past deeds, and thus show us how to master ourselves. The major emphasis is on how we can change ourselves by becoming conscious of our unconscious minds, for our will, united with God's, is more powerful than all the planetary influences."

Intrigued, I asked the Guides about John and his teacher at our next session, and they wrote: "John is from Arcturus. Frederick walked into his body a few years ago, coming directly from that star where he knew John. Frederick is a remarkable soul who has experienced every type of life on earth and on numerous planetary systems. He chose to come back because of an urgent need to reach the young people who will be founding the new society after the shift of the earth on its axis, and he is dedicated to his work. John will be of enormous aid to those who need counseling, because he is an old soul who taps into the universal wisdom. They were high priests in several previous incarnations, as they well know, and they are here this time to help awaken humanity before it is too late. They feel a destined role to help with the salvation of individuals and groups, and they are selfless in this task."

The Guides suggested that the two men should be included in this book, and when they came down from New York to see me, a surprise awaited.

John, who had written, and spoken on the telephone with such classic widom that I expected a man in his fifties, was only twenty-one years old. And because he had described Frederick as "a Hindu astrologer and lecturer," I was prepared to welcome a small, dark-complexioned man who would probably be wearing swami robes. Instead, I beheld the most beautiful specimen of manhood imaginable, with perfect features, sparkling blue eyes, blond hair, and a lithe physique garbed in preppy denims. And from the lips of this thirty-seven-year-old aristocrat poured a steady stream of loving philosophy that, if heeded by all humanity, could revolutionize the vibrations of planet earth.

He had been identified by my Guides as a Walk-in from another planet, and Frederick readily acknowledged it, saying, "Yes, it occurred in January of 1978. I came directly from Arcturus and am a totally different entity from the one that I replaced."

If so, the *New York Social Register* seems unaware of the fact. That venerable "bible" of elite society has continued to list Frederick Von Mierers, scion of an illustrious old New York family, who was reared at 68th Street and Park Avenue, within its "hallowed" pages. The "new" Frederick, who has an apartment in New York's East Fifties and a delightful "cottage" in the most desirable section of Nantucket, seems totally uninterested in the glamorous life led by his predecessor in that handsome body. He doesn't even like to talk about it, but Ruth Montgomery was not a newspaper reporter most of her adult life for nothing, and I gradually drew from him the following details:

The "old" Frederick, born on Christmas day in 1946, was four years old when his parents died in an automobile accident. Although officially reared by grandparents, he spent most of his time thereafter in the company of his godmother, Mrs. Earle Kress Williams, a member of the State Department Fine Arts Committee and niece of Samuel H. Kress, the noted merchant and philanthropist, who was a trustee of the Metropolitan Museum of Art in New York and of the National Gallery of Art in Washington, to the latter of which he donated his fabulous Kress collection of Italian paintings and sculpture.

In company with his dowager godmother, Frederick traveled the high roads of Europe, meeting socially with the Queen of England and European aristocracy, and mingling freely in the social life of Newport, Southampton, Nantucket, and Oyster Bay, New York, where they resided on Cove Road. Frederick says that he realized "even then" that Helen Williams had been his mother in several previous lifetimes, and they were almost inseparable.

"She knew everyone," Frederick remarked. "She launched my career in architecture and design; I was associated with decorators Billy Baldwin and David Hicks, the son-in-law of Lord Mountbatten. Yet she was deeply spiritual, as was I, and I often left parties in Venice, Rome or Paris to go home alone and study our books on Edgar Cayce and Eastern philosophy. She didn't mind. She understood perfectly."

Because of his exceptional good looks, Frederick also became a widely sought-after male model, and Fritz Diekmann, the top representative in North and South America for a huge German television conglomerate, told me that when he first knew Frederick "you could see him on practically every billboard in Western Europe." He was a free, fun-loving young man who saw no evil in anything or anybody.

The charmed life of the "old" Frederick came to an abrupt halt during the mid-seventies when a drunken driver in a stolen car struck the limousine of Mrs. Earle Kress Williams, as she was leaving an exclusive country club on Long Island one afternoon. She suffered a debilitating stroke, and although Frederick waged a successful battle to prevent her from being placed in a rest home, a battle in which he was backed by distinguished attorney Eustace Seligman, some of his friends turned against him. Deeply hurt, he contracted a severe streptococcal infection, and in 1977 Mrs. George Vanderbilt flew him to California for specialized treatment. His body gradually began to mend, but he remained in a deeply depressed state, "seeing the emptiness of it all, disenchanted with the world, and wanting out," he says.

Then, in January of 1978 the bewildering substitution of egos apparently occurred. Alone in his New York bedroom, the "new" Frederick saw himself being buried alive in a sarcophagus, to overcome fear of death, as part of the initiation in becoming a high priest in Egypt. In vivid flashes he recollected his life as a mathematician and astrologer involved in building the Egyptian pyramid at Giza, and another incarnation at the time of Buddha in India.

"During the next seven days, three beings materialized before me in my room, and deep secrets were revealed to me," he said. "Overnight I became an adept in the science of Hindu astrology. I knew that I had come from Arcturus, where I had lived in a hydrogen-light body, and I knew why I had come back. I was aware that a young man I'd known on Arcturus would be coming to assist me in the work, and in a series of visions I saw the coming wars, the destruction of New York City, my own mission, and the future of the earth.'' He says that he shut himself away from everyone for six months. Then he sold all of his antiques and luxurious furnishings, divested himself of his social connections, and dedicated himself to a life of service to humanity.

At this point I asked the Guides whether the above summary was factual, and they wrote: ''The account by Frederick is basically correct, and occurred at that time when his predecessor was overcome with heartbreak at what seemed to be the treachery of friends, and remorse for a life that he felt to have been wasted on frivolities. The present Frederick was an old adept in ancient India, as was John Andreadis, and both were high priests who went through the Egyptian initiation in the temple. Frederick was one of those who helped to plan and begin erection of the Giza pyramid, and John was with him in that lifetime. Arcturus is without atmosphere as we earthlings know it, but is a wonderful growth area for soul improvement. We were there, and know it to be a divine inspiration to all who inhabit those light bodies and who move freely with and through each other, melding with others in the radiance of pure love.''

Inasmuch as the lives of Frederick and John now begin to converge, let us take up the story from the vantage point of John Andreadis, who was born in New York City to a Jewish mother and Greek Orthodox father, although both were nonpracticing and gave no religious training to their son. John nevertheless began at the age of six to read the Bible for several hours each night.

"I had never been to a church service or syna-
gogue," he says, "but I instinctively loved God,
and as I read the parables of Jesus I felt deep
insight into their meaning. At the age of ten, alone
and despairing because no one seemed to share my
interest, I prayed, 'Oh Father, what should I do?'
At that moment I saw two large hands folded in
prayer against the window curtains, and knew that
all I had to do was pray to serve. The next night, in
a shaft of golden light I saw Jesus in a white robe
walk across my bedroom and out the window,
disappearing in a blaze of light. A day later I came
home from school and told my mother that I was
not Jewish. 'But of course you're Jewish,' she
replied, and I contradicted her, saying, 'I can't be
Jewish, because I believe in Jesus and want to be
just like him.'

"At the age of eleven I bought a book on Hatha
Yoga, and began meditating with a mantra. A year
later, while in the kitchen I saw Lord Krishna in
three-dimensional form, even to his blue-black hair,
red lips and a dark mole. I rubbed my eyes vigor-
ously, but when I reopened them he was still there,
raising his hand in benediction, and I felt overwhelmed with love and ecstasy. That's when I sold
my stereo set and bought the Hindu harmonium,
and for four or five hours each night I meditated
and chanted in my room. I had my own religion of
great love, but I couldn't share my feelings with
others. I knew and loved every one in our whole
area of New York City—all the jocks and preps
and grown-ups—and I was a hit at every party, but
I had no one to talk to about the most important
thing in my life."

At the age of fourteen he met Rob, a boy three
years older than himself who also meditated, and

who practiced spiritual healing. They began communicating telepathically when apart, and Rob confided that he was a student of a remarkable astrologer named Frederick, but could not introduce them because his parents had forbidden further contact. John began praying for the Christ Consciousness to come into his life, and one evening he had a deep spiritual experience. "I saw the universe filled with a golden-pink light that was healing the earth of all disease and evil," he recounted, "and a voice said, 'I am God. You can only serve God through man.' I prayed, 'Father, please send me a teacher so that I can serve,' and at that moment I felt a baptism of spiritual light pouring through every cell in my body. Peace and love filled me, and I knew that my prayer had been heard."

Later, while meditating on his bed, he said that he saw as if watching a movie a boy in loincloth being led to sit on a tiger skin, and knew it to be himself. Then he relived snatches of previous lifetimes during the Italian renaissance, and in Greece and Egypt as a priest. In a flash he "knew that the I AM reincarnates—our essence but not our personalities—and I understood all."

It was after midnight when he excitedly telephoned his friend Rob to say, "I know that something amazing will happen to me today." After school he went to the Quest bookstore, and felt drawn to linger. Presently two men walked in, and when one of them asked for books by Paramahansa Yogananda, John suddenly blurted: "You're Frederick, aren't you!" The handsome stranger nodded, and when John told him that he was a friend of Rob's, he was given Frederick's address and telephone number and told that he could drop by.

Rapturous with joy, the two lads went together

that evening to Frederick's apartment, and when
John provided his birth date, Frederick responded,
"Yes, you are the one I've been waiting for."

At that moment, John says, "All of my dreams
came true. I had found my teacher, and my only
purpose in life became to serve humanity, to serve
God and man, and to become a better expression
of light. I was not quite fifteen years old, but from
then on I have studied and worked with Frederick.
I have deep understanding of the physics of the
universe—how everything works—that has been
given to me through recall of that life in a hydrogen-
light form-without-form on Arcturus. I have the
ability to tune in to inner forces and to understand
how extraterrestrial forces work. Anybody can
achieve this if he is willing to do the work—and
work and work."

Strangely, despite all of the hours that John devoted to prayer, meditation and yoga, his school
grades did not suffer. He was an excellent student
both in Riverdale country day school and at Brown-
ing Prep off Park Avenue at 62nd Street. He also
excelled at Columbia University and NYU, but at
the age of eighteen he forsook the ease of his
parents' life-style, with its servants and limousines,
to join Frederick in counseling and lecturing without pay, earning his own financial contribution by
waiting on tables in restaurants.

"My parents think I'm crazy," he says with a
grin. But he still remains on friendly terms with his
only sister, his mother, and the father who is a
distinguished and highly successful inventor of phar-
maceutical products, including the well-known Man
Tan that helped create the Palm Beach look year
round.

Frederick, who had sold his valuable possessions to finance his lecture tours and video tapes, explains that all of his needs are provided for. "Whatever happens, everything comes so long as you are serving God and mankind," he explains. "I'm one with the universe. I only accept as students young men and women who are clean-cut, clean living and hardworking. People who don't want to work or do anything contribute to soul degeneration through their self-indulgence. We must do the work, and love unconditionally. Most people are childish, but not childlike. They grow old, but they never grow up. We must never lose our Peter Pan quality, but fantasies become realities only through discipline. I sleep only three or four hours a night, and work twenty hours a day. If we eat the right food, and think the right thoughts, anyone can do that." Although he accepts no remuneration for his lectures on the Vedanta philosophy, even paying for his own travel expenses, and has spent seven hundred thousand dollars on the video tapes that are provided free to cable and television stations, he does charge for his astrological life readings, which he will do only for Walk-ins and serious seekers who want to turn their lives into more fruitful channels.

I have not had a reading by Frederick, but John says that they "cover past lives, complete psychological makeup, why we are as we are, our future, complete diet, and gem prescriptions, the major emphasis being on how we can change ourselves by becoming conscious of our unconscious minds." Frederick stresses the importance of wearing certain gem stones next to the skin, calling gems the chakra centers of the earth, or the "condensed light of God's own thoughts" which neutralize the "power of the dark side" to interfere with our spiritual development. He urged me to wear at all times my large topaz pendant, turned backward so that the stone instead of the gold mounting rests against my skin. But since the gold chain is fragile, and it is my favorite piece of evening jewelry I have not yet succumbed to his advice. My faithful readers are well aware of my native stubborn streak; but frankly I am thinking of buying a smaller topaz, sapphire and emerald, the three gems that he says I need to neutralize my own deficiencies, to wear beneath my dresses. Apparently he prescribes different stones for different people, depending on their personal needs, but he is not in the jewelry business, and does not sell them.

Frederick believes that his principal mission in returning to earth at this period is to "initiate the children and unite the Walk-ins," bringing them back to Christ Consciousness and speeding up their karma "so that they can get on with fulfilling their destiny." Of the Russian problem in today's war-torn world, he says, "I'm here to neutralize those evil forces that linger from the dark side of Atlantis and to change the energy of world leaders so that they can understand unconditional love for all beings."

"There is only one sin," he insists, "and that is to impose your will on another. Otherwise, life is a celebration, a costume ball, and at the close of each lifetime we shed our costume. I never married in Egypt, as a priest, and I will not do so in this incarnation. I teach my students that it is better not to indulge in sex, but rather to redirect that drive into spiritual growth, although the decision is theirs. Living an androgynous life leads to higher evolvement of the mind."

Frederick and John are vegetarians, and regular

partakers of herbs, but the former does not discourage his students from eating chicken and fish "during the seven-year period while their bodies are adjusting to the changeover" from being meat-eaters. He does not try to tell anyone what to do. He simply suggests. But he is eager to reach as many "wholesome" young people as possible, to help prepare them for the New Age that will be dawning about the year 2000, when inspired leadership will be required. And he feels that his time is short, because he believes that he will not be here for the shift of the earth on its axis near the end of this century.

In this, the Guides concur. When I asked them about some of Frederick's assertions, they wrote: "He states his mission properly. He will not be there for the shift. He will be removed in order to spare him for greater work on this side [the spirit plane] before he returns there to help with the building of the new society. Helen [Mrs. Earle Kress] Williams is ecstatic about Frederick and the work he is so successfully accomplishing." She passed on two years ago.

Because I was not personally convinced that John Andreadis had actually "seen" Krishna in the kitchen episode during his boyhood I also asked the Guides about that, and they wrote: "Krishna did appear to him, as he can do to all true believers who are ready to sacrifice a lifetime in service to humanity and who call fervently on him." But how many of us are willing to make that sacrifice, I wonder!

The summer before I made the acquaintance of these two Arcturians, Frederick was in line at the check-in counter of an airline in the Los Angeles airport when a college boy rushed in, saying that he simply had to get on the about-to-depart plane because it provided the only connection for his onward flight to Greece. There was only one remaining seat, which happened to be next to Frederick's, and the latter says that he "knew instantly" that this young man was a spiritual twin of John Andreadis. On reaching his apartment in New York he told John that he had met his "brother," and when Nicolas Chrissakis returned to America from his parents' home in Athens, to resume his computer science studies at Ohio University in Athens, Ohio, the two lads at last met.

John is Greek on his father's side, and they discovered numerous friends in common, both in New York and Athens. Nicolas is the son of a high-ranking Greek diplomat, whereas John's father is an industrial tycoon, but both had been accustomed to similar life-styles with wealthy parents. Amazingly, they had been born exactly one week apart in April 1963, although in widely separated countries; both were brilliant students who at an early age developed an overriding interest in spiritual development, shared nearly identical mannerisms and reactions, and had seemed mysteriously "led" to Frederick. Their rapport was instantaneous, and they now spend the Christmas and Easter vacations together.

At John's request I asked the Guides about them and their relation to Frederick, and they wrote: "Frederick spent quite a long while on Arcturus as earth time is reckoned, and became a shining soul who felt the call to preach the message of unconditional love to all mankind. In previous earth lives he had been a good and faithful servant of the Lord, serving as high priest in various religions, so that he realized on Arcturus that all are one, that

religions differ only in their outward forms, and
that in essence there is only one religion: the worship of God and the love of mankind. John was
there with him for some time, as was his twin,
Nicolas Chrissakis. When the twins decided to return to earth to live perfect lives, they arrived by
birth to different families, but both chose a Greek
connection because they had served as high initi-
ates in ancient Greece, and knew that they would
find each other again. They were *physical* twins
when both studied the Stoic philosophy in ancient
Greece, and they also sat at the feet of Socrates.
They are as like as two peas and had unconsciously
searched for each other throughout this present
lifetime. They are adepts of the highest order and
will wield great influence in the councils of state
during the decades ahead, more particularly after
the shift of the earth on its axis.''

They then discussed some others in the group
around Frederick, saying that they had known him
on Arcturus before returning to earth life through
the normal birth process, and added: ''Frederick
looked on with benevolence, and seeing the progress that they were making in overcoming past
errors, leading good and decent lives, and devoting
themselves to God and mankind he decided also to
return. But as he had been their leader in previous
lives he chose to come quickly into an adult body,
so that with greater awareness he might again find
and direct these glowing souls. Thus he came as a
Walk-in, to bring them all together again.''

I asked for more information about Arcturus,
and the Guides wrote: ''There is no atmosphere as
such there, but the souls who inhabit it have light
bodies needing no air to breathe and are able to
carry on their androgynous lives without tempta-

tions of the body. They are complete souls, neither male nor female, and they need no food or drink. They are Pure Soul, in other words; and we ourselves loved the atmosphere of devoted fellowship and would have remained longer, except that we feel a pressing need to assist earthlings through the difficult decades ahead, for we love the earth and its people. We will continue with this project [bringing guidance to earthlings] until the shift occurs, and perhaps shortly beyond that, and may then return there for a time in the beautiful period of rebuilding, when so much of the evil has been cleared away and the remaining and returning ones are obsessed only with love for each other and for God.''

I wanted to know the ways in which space people are entering our earth plane, and the Guides obligingly wrote: ''They are coming in great numbers to prepare earthlings for the coming shift, and while some are observers of the changes, and some are there to help clean up pollution, others are dedicated solely to leading earthlings along a higher path of development. They are more highly evolved, both spiritually and technologically, than earth people and have much to offer. They arrive in various ways. Some materialize from light bodies into human form, some land from spaceships, some replace souls wishing to depart, and arrive as Walk-ins. The transformation from light astral bodies into solid human bodies is not as difficult as it sounds to earthlings, who originally peopled the earth in just that fashion. They were thought forms in the mind of the Creator, then ethereal souls, then astral bodies, and finally in the earth plane they were in solid form. Some on other planetary systems are still in astral or ethereal bodies, coming and going as they please, and for them there is no difficulty in appearing on earth, as well as on Arcturus and other planets. They are thought forms and feel no barriers as they project themselves, the real I AM, to any locale.''

John Andreadis was unaware of this description by the Guides, but when I asked him to discuss our space friends he replied: "They don't come from the outside illusionary world of dense vibratory ice—matter is to spirit as ice is to water—but from within, from Paradise. We know that there is a speed limit to the objective world of matter, and that is 186,300 miles per second, the speed of light. However, this speed limit does not apply to the higher dimensional worlds where our space friends live. Don't confuse this fact with the quasar phenomenon NC273, because that is an entranceway from the higher dimension into this one, from a material point of view. The stars are the parents of matter. This is where the building blocks are made. However, NC273 is a focal point of higher dimensional light or intelligence which feeds this dimension with life. On the other side of this quasar is the vast sea of consciousness, not matter. It is from NC273 and other quasars like it that the Christ Consciousness or the Guiding Intelligent Force back of all forms fills this dimension with its power. Many space beings enter into this dimension through such doorways, but that is not the only way. And don't think that the Christ Consciousness, or the beings consciously attuned to it, are limited to that avenue of entrance alone, for in reality it enters through our minds and the hearts of each atom. It is omnipresent, transcendental in its scope.

"The source that supplies NC273 with its power is far beyond this dimension, and when this powerful force interacts with the matter of this dimension it quickens the vibrations of this dimension up to its limitation of light speed. Thus, everything in the way of this force is transmuted into light, or a higher form of energy according to its capacity to receive higher dimensional force. Therefore, it *appears* that light is moving at speeds beyond 186,300 m/sec., but this is impossible for light of this dimension, and is not the case. Light is *not* moving beyond its speed limit, but the energy from NC273 *is*. That is the secret! The energy that Swedish scientist Björn Örtenheim calls Super Plasma is force or energy, but it vibrates much faster than physical light and consequently can travel through space more quickly. It is this higher octave of energy that acts as the controlling force of intelligence known in this dimension as Universal Consciousness. However, do not limit the Christ Power only to Super Plasma, for this impersonal force transcends all the worlds and is worthy of our humble worship. Our intelligence is just an infinitesimal part of His intelligence. We are created from Him, out of Him, by Him.''

I broke in to ask what all of this had to do with extraterrestrials, and John said: ''Our brothers and sisters from outer space come from this higher realm of existence, which is really inner space. Some do also inhabit bodies composed of material from this dimension, but those who do are able to ascend in consciousness to this higher, impersonal realm and rematerialize at any point in the physical universe that they desire. It is beyond the place called 'the other side' where our departed loved ones go, for this higher realm can only be entered consciously, free from the throes of death. There are different classes of extraterrestrials now coming to this planet for various reasons. Many are coming only to observe the crucial transition of our race from the Piscean to the Aquarian Age, but many more are coming with a definite purpose to take an active role in helping earthlings prepare for this transition. It must be remembered that although we are many souls dwelling on many planets and stars throughout many dimensions of conscious unfoldment, we all share a single parent who is God. There is only one God, who is Love. We cannot claim Jesus, Rama, Krishna, Buddha or the other avatars as our own. Their greatness embraces the entire cosmos. These concepts must be understood if we are to grasp the meaning of the advent of our space brothers and sisters and know how to greet them. First we are souls, children of God. Then we may become earthlings, Venusians, Arcturians, etc. Different souls incarnate on different planets to experience the various vibratory lessons that can be learned on each planet. There are many souls evolving through matter, but only the most advanced races of this dimension have understood the secrets of intergalactic or interdimensional travel. Only the great Yogis of this planet (one of whom was Jesus Christ) have understood how to do it, and the Hindu Vedas give elaborate descriptions of all the planets and star systems, not only of this universe but of the astral and causal planes, and the beings who inhabit them.

"Paramahansa Yogananda described these facts in his book, *Autobiography of a Yogi*, but only recently have these ideas been dreamed of in the West, and that is because of the leap in awareness that our planet is undergoing. As the vibratory rate of human consciousness increases, so does our capacity to receive and attune ourselves to the sacred Aum vibration, which is the Holy Ghost, the forerunner of the emancipating Christ Consciousness. Because of this increased vibration of human consciousness we are more able to attune ourselves to the higher intelligences from other dimensions, and they are able to contact those of us who are receptive.''

John said that one day ''in a flash it was given'' to him that without the presence of Babaji and his spiritual family on this planet, many souls of high spiritual standing would not be able to incarnate here from other planetary systems without tremendous struggle to maintain spiritual balance, because of the intense discord on planet earth. In India, Babaji is called Mahavatar, The Great Incarnation, and his presence was first revealed to the Western world in 1946 through Paramahansa Yogananda's *Autobiography of a Yogi,* which described him as the ''deathless avatara'' and declared that ''the secluded Master has retained his physical form for centuries, perhaps for millennia'' in order to uplift humanity.

John says of Babaji: ''This Master is fully merged with God, and is known as the Supreme Servant. His presence creates a tremendous spiritual polarization that establishes a strong field of righteousness and harmony about the earth plane. This polarization creates a tremendous spiritual attraction for all good souls to come here. Thus, by Babaji's mere presence on this plane many other great souls and lovers of God are enabled to come here, for I assure you that were it not for the presence of Babaji none of us would be able to stand the intense discord of this plane. Babaji promised that he would not leave his physical body until the end of this particular world cycle, and we should all be grateful for the tremendous sacrifice that he has undertaken for the children of the earth.''

Although I had read about Babaji many years ago in Yogananda's autobiography, my face must have reflected my doubts at John's sweeping claim, because he urged me to consult the Guides about his assertion. On doing so, the Guides wrote as follows: "Babaji is indeed in flesh whenever he chooses to exercise his right to the body that continues to flourish in India. He is a source of wonderment to those who are privileged to meet him. Space people are aware of his existence and are drawn to him as moths to a flame, but there would be some dissension if they all flocked to India, and not to the Western world where the leadership currently rests and the need is greatest for benevolence and understanding of all peoples. These space friends are materializing in every part of the world now, and are able to do so without the machines [UFOs] that caused too much discussion and idle curiosity, and they are visible to any who wish to see them, for they can assume the shape of skin and bones and walk among us, although they are also required to materialize identification papers and background material if they want to work and function in today's society. But this necessity is obviated if they arrive as Walk-ins, to replace a soul that wishes to depart.''

This dissertation prompted me to begin rereading my well-worn copy of *Autobiography of a Yogi*, and on a day when I asked the Guides to tell me what has become of him since his physical death, they wrote: "Yogananda is an avatara who now freely comes and goes as he pleases, and is sometimes with Babaji in the Himalayas. The latter's physical body is kept alive through fresh air, sunlight and spiritual repast, for he seldom eats other than occasional nectar and water. These Completed Ones who have worked off all karma need not replenish themselves with earthly food unless they so choose.''

I was well aware that the late Arthur Ford, now a member of the spirit group that writes through me, had once studied under Yogananda, and that after the latter's death in 1952 in Los Angeles, Harry T. Rowe, mortuary director of Forest Lawn Memorial Park in Glendale, California, sent Yogananda's devoted followers a notarized letter that said in part: "The absence of any visual signs of decay in the dead body of Paramahansa Yogananda offers the most extraordinary case in our experience. No physical disintegration was visible in his body even twenty days after death. No indication of mold was visible on his skin, and no visible desiccation took place in the bodily tissues. This state of perfect preservation of a body is, so far as we know from mortuary annals, an unparalleled one. At the time of receiving Yogananda's body, the mortuary personnel expected to observe, through the glass lid of the casket, the usual progressive signs of bodily decay. Our astonishment increased as day followed day without bringing any visible change in the body under observation. Yogananda's body was apparently in a phenomenal state of immutability. No odor of decay emanated from his body at any time. The appearance of Yogananda on March 27, just before the bronze cover of the casket was put into position, was the same as it had been on March 7. He looked on March 27 as fresh and as unravaged by decay as he had looked on the night of his death. On March 27 there was no reason to say that his body had suffered any visible physical disintegration at all. For these reasons we state again that the case of Paramahansa Yogananda is unique in our experience.''

Apparently since Yogananda was not really of the earth, having been born here (in India) only after many sojourns in other planetary systems, it was unnecessary for his body to become "ashes to ashes and dust to dust." Like Swami Vivekananda, who through his address to the Parliament of Religions held in Chicago in 1893, and his subsequent lectures throughout America, England and France was the first to electrify Westerners to the fountain of ancient wisdom in the Hindu religion, Yogananda helped build the spiritual bridge between East and West. Thanks to the shining efforts of these two trailblazers from India, the minds of Westerners were finally opened to the now widespread belief in reincarnation and karma.

John Andreadis agrees with my Guides that souls from other planets have always been present here, but he asserts that until recently the mass consciousness of the human race was so dense and matter-bound that we could not contact them. "Now many souls from other stars and planets are able to incarnate here and to experience the vibrations of earth," he says, "because the earth is passing through a higher electro-spiritual field known as the Aquarian constellation. It is due to this higher influx of light vibration that we are even able to understand the fact of NC273.''

Alas, I am not one of those who has the faintest inkling of what the formula is all about. I hope John was not referring directly to me, however, when he continued: "These increased vibrations are also causing all the matterbound souls who are not able to glimpse beyond the veil of sense perceptions to go a little crazy. This is because all of these new energies are out of 'sync' with the lower sense-mad mind. That is why the pole shift will come to liberate them from this plane and to liberate the spiritually minded from them.''

Jeepers! No wonder the Guides have told me that I will not be around for the shift of the earth on its axis at the end of this century. I'm apparently one of those dullards from whom the Aquarian age needs to be "liberated."

I asked John to explain what he was talking about in terms that even I could understand, and this twenty-one-year-old Arcturian replied: "When a cold-water fish is placed in warm water it will die. The Piscean age through which we have been passing since the time of Christ is a water sign, symbolic of cold water; yet the Aquarian age deals with electromagnetic waves of higher vibrations and of the higher vibration of water, which is steam. Aquarius is a gaseous or air sign, so all souls acclimated only to liquid water cannot survive in the higher, more spiritual electromagnetic waters of truth. We are transcending an octave in consciousness, and only one out of twenty-five souls now incarnated on this planet will be able to stand these higher vibrations. The space visitors are naturally acclimated to the higher vibration of the Christ Consciousness and are here to help usher mankind into a new golden age, dedicated to the worship of our One Father through all aspects of life.''

I timorously asked why and how we could presently be "transcending an octave in consciousness," and he declared that the earth is now in the portion of its 24,000-year orbit in which it is moving closer to the galactic center, or seat of God.

"The galactic center is the focal point of God's energy in this galaxy," he continued, "as it is the magnetic point around which the central suns rotate, and is the most powerful source of energy in our system. Thus the vibrations of the atomic structure are increasing, and with this increased vibratory rate humanity as a whole is becoming increasingly more aware of the subtler states of matter like radio waves, X rays, electromagnetic waves and the like. What this means is that humanity is becoming aware of the finer forces in nature, and thus is more able to comprehend the possibility of higher dimensional realities that in actuality are the homelands of the various extraterrestrial intelligences. As modern physics has proven, all of life is vibration. As we grow spiritually we become conscious of an entire universe that transcends the limited realm of the five senses. It transcends duality, and everything in it is conscious.

"These are the higher dimensional worlds and star systems that are inhabited by superterrestrial intelligences. The bodies of our space brothers and sisters are not as dense or tangible as ours. They are more like thought projections. Though many of them come from planets in this solar system, the most advanced come from farther-away systems that serve as training schools for souls. If a soul is to enter into a new solar system it must be trained in the ways of that system so that it can be of greatest service to the race. When souls finally free themselves from earth they go to Arcturus before leaving our system, where they receive training before going on to higher ideals of service. Many of our space friends here are those who have gone on from this world in Mastery, and then come back to serve and participate in the great plan for the salvation of the earth."

John says that our space friends travel the universe on beams of light or astral planes, and materialize a spaceship or a body when they reach their destination. "Their travel is interdimensional, and they come in forms according to the vibrations of their recipient environment," he explains. "Just as your Guides can perceive this dimension where we are, but we cannot perceive them, so do our space friends perceive us without being perceived by us, unless they want us to, in which case they materialize bodies and spaceships to experience the fullness of this dimension. Many people on earth are having extraterrestrial contact either physically, or in dream state, or telepathically.

"They *are* here, and they will become known. Many great discoveries are to be made with their help in the near future, just as was done on the lost continents of Atlantis and Lemuria. The earth is part of an intergalactic universe-federation of which we have been ignorant for over twelve thousand years. The Ascended Masters and higher dimensional beings have never lost touch with us, though we in our indulgent pursuits became so engrossed in dense matter-consciousness that we lost touch with our friends who are beyond the five-senses world. Now all this is changing with the advent of the Aquarian age."

Although John was unaware of the material that I have gathered from Dr. Hynek and Dr. Sprinkle about extraterrestrial visitations, he is here expressing the precise opinion of those outstanding scientist-educators: that the UFO phenomenon is both physical and psychical. The spacecraft and the space people are indeed real, but at this point it depends on them, whether they wish us to see and touch and talk with them verbally, or through mental telepathy.

CHAPTER EIGHT

Philosophy From Arcturus

FREDERICK Von Mierers and John Andreadis spent much of the summer of 1984 in California, training young leaders for the arduous decades ahead. John flew back briefly to see me, and during that second visit I was again astounded by the philosophy and esoteric wisdom that pour from this twenty-one-year-old Arcturian, far too rapidly for my pencil to take down the proper notes. Because his views and those of Frederick are synonymous, I ventured to ask whether he would be willing to write out for me what they both felt would be important to include in this book about extraterrestrials.

The amiable young man gladly assented, and a week or so later I received in the mail, not a few paragraphs, but nineteen hand-printed pages! It was then I learned that this genius from outer space has not yet learned to type on an earthly machine.

As I began to read the voluminous material, I became increasingly aware that it had enormous value, but that it might put some of my readers, including myself, to sleep. It was too long to swallow in one piece, yet I saw no way, without breaking the continuity, to cut it into more edible bites.

At last, despairing of arriving at a solution to the problem, I consulted the Guides, who commented on the lengthy material as follows: "It is all factual. It is true. Do not worry about giving too big a chunk of it at a time, as the readers will avidly consume it. A whole new dimension of thought for them!"

Since I could think of no better solution myself, I hereby reproduce the material that John sent me from Frederick and himself.

John and Frederick Write

In order to gain a deeper understanding of our space brothers and sisters, what they look like, where they live and how they travel, we must understand some basic metaphysical principles. First we must know that in back of the physical manifestation of one or more of the five vibratory elements, behind all material forms, there is a guiding force: a spiritual impulse of superconscious Intelligence which determines the forms of all things. In God all things are conscious.

Our scientists can trace the law of cause and effect all the way back to the subatomic particles, but beyond that they have no reckoning. Herein lies room for the emergence of a divine Intelli-

gence, an Intelligence which determines the arrangement of particles to form the various chemical elements that form the foundation of our material world. In reality things are not at all as they appear, because the physical cosmos is nothing more than the union of intelligence with substance. Thus we are dealing with a universe of vibratory action. Everything is energy. Do not think that life is bound to five vibrations of sensory perception, for it is much more. As we become more subtlized in our consciousness we begin to perceive more rarified octaves of energy and light. Everything is life. Everything is alive with consciousness.

We must realize that the distance between the atoms in our bodies (atoms being building blocks of all matter) is exactly proportional to the distance between the stars. In other words, if we take two atoms and multiply them to the size of stars, the ratio of the distances between is the same. But when we observe the life in our bodies, where does it exist? Only in the heart? Or brain? Or lungs? Of course not. Life is present everywhere in our bodies. That is why if someone touches any part of your body you can feel it. Now, do you limit the life in your bodies to a cell or an organ? Or do you say that life is a universalized presence in the body? It is, upon thinking, universalized. That is why all living bodies radiate heat. Furthermore, do you think that the life is limited to each atom, or is it the cohesive force which connects the atoms? It must connect the atoms, otherwise why would they disintegrate upon the transition called death? Therefore life spans the space between the atoms.

Taking this concept to the next logical conclusion, is it so difficult to realize that since the relative distances between atoms and between stars *are the same, that life permeates interstellar spaces as it does the interatomic spaces? Lastly, don't scientists realize that what they call plasma is the same as body heat? It is, and this will become a major scientific discovery that will prove the existence of what we call God. This is the explanation of Christ (Rama, Krishna, Buddha) Consciousness. Just as you are the supreme consciousness in relation to the mini-consciousness of each cell in your body, so is Christ the Supreme Consciousness in relation to the mini-consciousness of our egos. An avatar or liberated soul is one who is identified with the Supreme Consciousness and thus is omnipresent. This is the state that we call God. But there is a state beyond that, and that is the state beyond the body whether it be physical or universal. That is the supreme "I" existing in the vibrationless void beyond creation—unqualified Being—unqualified nondualism that the Hindus call Paramatman.*

With this in mind, we realize that all apparent individuals are only expressions of one individual—I AM. This I AM is life. It is pure unqualified energy, and whenever the I AM contacts matter, the matter is activated and comes alive. Thus, because our space friends and the ascended masters exhibit a greater degree of I AM identification than most humans, they inhabit higher vibrational worlds and are able to live in multidimensional consciousness. Their presence proves that souls were not meant to be bound in the physical vibrations of any planet; but if they realize who they are, they can manifest perfect freedom.

Many space friends are coming into the vibratory field of earth and do so according to various means. The highest are the ascended Masters and those in their charge. There are many space broth-ers and sisters that travel in huge motherships on beams of light. Many of them are from other gal-axies and from star systems within this galaxy. Lastly, there are many souls who never became entangled in this earth system, but who have re-ceived cosmic training in different, higher vibra-tional spheres. Among these souls, many are sacrificing their great freedom and actually incar-nating physically onto this planet, or becoming Walk-ins. Keep in mind, however, that those who do so have been training on Sirius and in other star systems to contend with the dense, misqualified vibratory energies of this extreme world of oppo-sites. Those who incarnate from the latter class have usually had one or two or more "practice" incarnations at different points in earth's recent history—meaning within the last 10,000 years.

The earth and her solar system are reaching the end of a grand cycle of the ages. This is much greater than the cycle of 24,000 years that we mentioned previously, and its culmination will re-sult in the graduation of countless souls into the permanent awareness of the great I AM. There-fore, this is a cosmic event that the hierarchies of angels and masters have been preparing for, for aeons. This epochal transition coincides with the passage of the Piscean into the Aquarian age. The Aquarian constellation represents the powerful, spir-itually charged waves of electromagnetic and spiri-tual energies bombarding the earth and transforming the vibrations of all things moving, living, breath-ing, or merely sitting upon her. All energy is being transmuted to a higher frequency. Therefore, only souls who are able to stand these new energies will be able to remain on the planet as we pass into the year 2000.

The transition may be visualized as such: both Pisces and Aquarius represent water. Pisces represents the emotional waters of personal human feelings. The Piscean emotions are based entirely upon subject-object dualities and opposites. It is either positive or negative and is always a manifestation of reaction—I do this, you feel that. Thus the symbol of Pisces is indicative of tension, the inability to reconcile opposites. In order to master this tension we must learn to walk on water like Jesus, or if you will, we must learn to balance the emotional energies and transcend duality in our minds.

Remember, all thoughts of anger, jealousy, irritation, deceit, fear and other negative emotions are only reactions to circumstances that appear in the outer world. Thus our mental states depend upon how we react. No one is forced to be angry or irritated, but these states of thought-energy become encoded into our mental structures by repeated indulgence in them, and they thus become habits. All of these negative emotional habits keep our souls earthbound in a self-created ego prison with bars molded out of thoughts. Any limitations that we perceive are only in our minds. Change your thoughts and you change your life. This is the Great Law. Our space friends are proof of this.

What are you? Not what you think! Your outer reality or personality is what you think, but you are not that. Your outer self is a vehicle for your self-expression and you are eternal. You are that which watches your thoughts pass through your mind. You are I AM, the eternal uncreated silent watcher. You are pure unqualified life, the I AM that causes the heart to beat, the lungs to breathe, the food to digest. Through the presence of consciousness, which you are, dumb matter speaks and appears to be alive. By identifying with our thoughts, which are none other than qualified vibrations of life energy, we become attached to a particular reality pattern. But remember: First I AM, then I act. Your attention is your divine director. Let it be free. By freeing our attention from limitation we are able to attune to any thought vibration that we desire, and that will become our outer reality. In order to free our attention from limitation we must simply tune in or contemplate the great I AM presence, our own true selves. This I AM is beyond thought and is the only power. Think of this day and night and you will be free. This is the message of our space friends who have ascended in their consciousness to this state.

Aquarius represents the infiltration of limited thought patterns with unlimited I AM awareness. Aquarius represents the spiritual waters of truth flowing out of the chalice of divine consciousness. It represents the higher octaves of vibration of electromagnetic energy, which corresponds to radio, television, astrology, telepathy and the divine sciences. It is energy infused with Christ Consciousness. It is the new dispensation given to humanity in order better to understand its origin and destiny. The secrets of energy are revealed in Aquarius, and mankind will make tremendous strides forward in this field. Aquarius is an air sign, but it is based upon watery air, gas, or energy waves. Energy waves travel through space unhindered, as do our souls and consciousness when we free ourselves from earthly limitations. Thus, Aquarius reveals our future 2,000 years, just as we are leaving the Piscean age after 2,000 years.

With all this going on, is it any wonder that we have spectators? Our space friends have come to help. Not to help an alien civilization, but to help their brothers and sisters. We are all souls with a divine Parent who is God. First I AM, then I ACT. Souls in the beginning were free to act according to their desires. All souls in the beginning acted in harmony with the Divine Will and never became attached to what they thought. They simply experienced their thoughts as a Divine Play. But as time progressed, many souls became attached to their Play and became entrapped in various systems of thought vibrations which ultimately evolved into planets, stars, solar systems, galaxies, and ultimately infinite island universes. All of this occurred in the mind of God, the Supreme Cosmic Dreamer.

God is the supreme and final I AM. God is the all-invisible realm of thoughts from which everything comes and into which everything must return. God in His aspect of Creator is the original thinker and the original thought. That is why there is only one law present throughout the entire system of universes. All has progressed according to His plan. Even we are only His ideas in action, and as such have no ultimate individuality except as Him. According to the degree that we are unattached to circumstances and phenomena, we can roam freely to different star systems and universes in the physical, astral (or thought) and causal (or ideational) worlds.

Though many space beings, who are only souls like us that inhabit thought-worlds, actually incarnate here in the normal fashion, some walk into full-grown bodies, others are beamed down from spaceships, which are only thought-ships that materialize as they enter into this dimension, and still others come here by mental projection. The highest are the ascended Masters who are free from all limitation and can be anywhere they like in an instant. These Great Ones merge into omnipresence and emerge wherever they like through the simplest technique of identification. Anyone who can grasp what is about to be discussed is getting a glimpse into his own future. For this is the destiny of every soul everywhere, to be like Jesus, the great Yogi-Christs of India, and the ascended Masters, all of whom exhibit the same awareness through identification with the omnipresent I AM consciousness.

No one is from this planet. Everyone is from God, or consciousness. Everyone on earth is actually a space being, but no one comes from outer space. Really we come from inner space. All that we are are thoughts. This means that all concept of separation and personality is thought, but our consciousness which is the I AM is what animates these thoughts and is beyond thought. Thought itself comes and goes. We experience an idea and it passes. But our consciousness does not come and go, it remains ever the witness to these thoughts.

What is thought? It is energy and vibration that are like waves that rise and fall. God is the still ocean of I AM awareness, and the energy waves on His surface are the creation. All the waves exist in the ocean, and when they rise they become manifest; when they fall they are unmanifest. An ascended Master or Yogi does not identify with any particular wave, but merges into the Supreme Identity and emerges at any point he desires. Thus, his travel is instant. The original souls who inhabited earth, known as Sons of God, shared this

knowledge. They too came from space, and differ-
ent planets. This is an open-ended universe.

Now we are going to share with you some knowledge about ourselves and our planet. Where do
you think Adam and Eve came from? Go in your
minds back to the beginning of humanity—humanity
as we know it from a spiritual, metaphysical view-
point. Let's go back before Atlantis and Lemuria,
before the advent of the Sons of God. Do not be
confused if I speak of Adam and Eve as individuals, for many know that they represent humanity.
However, as the first individuals, how did they get
here? Five minutes before their advent the earth
was quiet, and they arrived with a quiet humming
sound, the sound of vibrating electrons. They did
not come by spaceship, as some may think, because that is a useless machine to a free soul,
unless he simply wants to enjoy the idea of a
spaceship. He doesn't need it to move from place
to place. Actually, they materialized right out of
the ether, and the sound of the atoms arranging
themselves into human form created a hum.

The original humanity was divine. Of course we
are too, but you can say that we are fallen angels,
ignorant of our true estate. However, our true
ancestors were gods. Even Jesus said so. The Sons
of God came from heaven to incarnate into the
earth. But let's go back to the original creation
and understand what is the substance of creation.
Creation is essentially the union of intelligence
with substance. The great Yogis Paramahansa
Yogananda and Swami Vivekananda were the first
to reveal these secrets to the Western world. Both
physics and Yoga philosophy describe a Big Bang
or an initial point of creative outlet which expanded
into the physical cosmos. The Yogis say that in the

beginning was the Word (yes, that is actually a Hindu concept) and the Word was with God, and the Word was God. The Word is the sacred Aum vibration, the creative intelligent force that guides creation. All forms, thoughts, entities, ideas and concepts emerge from Aum, and Aum is omnipresent. As St. John said, without Him was not one thing made that was made. Aum is both the structure of creation and the intelligent force guiding creation, and this is the basis of awareness.

Behind every creative form is its astral blueprint, or the thought of which it is a manifestation. This thought is energy, but as an idea it is eternal. The Akashic Records are the records of these eternal thoughts that have at one time or another found manifestation in the physical cosmos. Just as we tune a radio to different stations or frequency bands, so we can attune our consciousness to any thought in the universe. Spiritual thoughts are those of the highest frequency and give the most "listening pleasure." Thus, we can conceive of a universe created out of thought that exists beyond this physical cosmos and which feeds it with energy.

It is the physical atoms which, through polarization, attach themselves to a particular astral blueprint that form planets. That is what is meant by gravity. Gravity causes all matter to be attracted to an invisible center. Were it not for the essential resistance in matter, matter would be absorbed into this point and disappear. But since there is resistance, different forms can coagulate about these invisible points and form worlds.

Do not forget, however, that we are still dealing with energy and energy forms in patterns. There is really no such thing as solid substance. Matter is only condensed energy or thought. Whatever you think, you attract and become. Thought is the basis of creation. Thus the mass consciousness determined by the sum total of all thoughts experienced by all the souls on a particular planet determines the mass karma of that planet and that race. This also applies to nations, religions, cities, families or groups of any kind.

Furthermore, every soul is marked by the signature of his particular vibration, which exhibits a color, a tone and a pattern. This vibration is determined by the thoughts and feelings that he experiences. A group of souls in harmony, all being polarized to a spiritual ideal, will create a symphony among themselves. This symphony is created by mutual service and cooperation. However, if souls of a self-seeking, self-indulgent nature come together they create cacophony or discord. If strong enough, this discord can destroy an entire planet.

That is the crisis that we face on earth. Our planet receives its life from the cosmic Source through certain energy grids. It is like a radio. However, the mass karma of humanity is such that we create so much discord that the pattern which sustains this planet is being disintegrated by our disruptive energies. Just as when there is static on the radio, we cannot bring in a station, so do our thoughts create enough static to drown the energy received from the Source. This does not mean that the initial energy is not being sent, but it is being absorbed by discord.

This phenomenon is another reason why space beings are coming to our aid. I know it sounds farfetched, but they are able to amplify the cosmic energy necessary to revivify the etheric blueprint of our planet and sustain it. This is done by concentrating energies of harmony and peace to the most discordant areas. When this is not possible, the great cosmic beings effect minor earth changes on the surface of the planet to release tension. When the tension is more of a psychological nature it erupts in war. That is why the presence of Babaji, as noted earlier, is so important to the well-being of earthly humanity.

To say all of this another way, our body is the earth, our mind is the astral blueprint of the earth, our soul is the causal plane of ideas that feed the astral plane with life. God is the source of our soul and the supreme I AM. God is unqualified life energy—the I AM THAT I AM.

When there is too much discord in our body, our body dies, and our soul and mental bodies move on. Let's not make our presence on this earth cancerous and kill its physical body. When we establish high mental ideals we can conquer discord and destruction in our body. That is the task of the disciple. When we polarize our mind to the I AM, to the soul, we eradicate all mental inharmony and establish mental and spiritual illumination. That is the service rendered by Babaji to humanity. When this spiritual identification is achieved, all souls may move on into the eternal freedom of cosmic consciousness and the eternal joy of being with God, the supreme I AM, everywhere on every planet throughout eternity at the same time.

It is true that our space brothers and sisters have arrived. And we are they!

CHAPTER NINE

Frederick's Arcturian Friends

THE next time that John Andreadis came down from New York he brought with him Fritz Diekmann, senior vice-president of one of the world's largest television conglomerates, who represents all of its interests in the Western hemisphere, buying, producing and selling television productions. Because I knew that he was coming, I asked the Guides about Fritz and they wrote: "He is one of the adepts who worked among the Hindu and Moslem elements of India a long time ago. He is steeped in Hindu philosophy and is of a high order indeed. He is, of course, from Arcturus."

Curious to know how such a highly successful executive could have become a "student" of Frederick Von Mierers, I drew him out about himself, and learned that he was born in Germany during

World War II, had his schooling and training there, and is an officer in the West German Air Force Reserve. He lived in England, France, and for another five years in Munich before moving to the United States in 1974. It was during those years in Munich that he met Frederick. A friend returning from a trip to Italy excitedly reported that he had met an extraordinary person in Venice who would shortly be arriving in Munich. He came, and Fritz said that he was unusually impressed by the "discipline, directness, openness and honesty of the charismatic young man," at that time a professional model for the Ford Agency, who was also deeply interested in spiritual development and astrology.

"Frederick was traveling in Europe a great deal at the time," Fritz recalled, "and when in Munich he would stay with me. It was the only time I've had a house guest who traveled with a suitcase full of books instead of clothes. Most of the books were about Edgar Cayce, and there was also a fat black book called *Ephemerus* in which Frederick became absorbed every night. It was all totally mysterious to me. All I knew was that he was doing a lot of checking and cross-checking, and occasionally would slam shut the astrology book, saying, 'Well, child, the stars have moved and so must I.' Then he would move on."

Fritz said that their paths did not often cross during the ensuing years. "After I moved to New York ten years ago," he explained, "I was busy with my career and with burning the candle at both ends. Our pursuits were running in opposite directions, and as a result my contact with Frederick was only negligible. Curiously, it was the same friend who originally introduced us in Munich who reestablished our friendship. After a visit of several weeks in New York during 1982, he was preparing to return to Germany when he expressed a desire to see Frederick again. The three of us went out together, and in the weeks that followed I occasionally hung out at Frederick's apartment with all the young people who kept regularly showing up there, slowly becoming intrigued by an approach to life that was unfamiliar to me. [This was, of course, the 'new' Frederick who had become a Walk-in four years earlier.]

"Before long Frederick did a life reading for me, and I remember it like yesterday. I arrived at his apartment at three o'clock one Friday afternoon, and because I had not yet had lunch, John fixed me a watercress salad. Then I was plugged into the tape recorder for my life reading, and for ninety minutes I could hardly believe what I was hearing. Afterwards I returned to my office, but the first colleague I ran into asked if I was all right, because my face was as white as a sheet. To be quite honest, I felt lousy and was afraid of fainting, so I grabbed my briefcase and had the colleague accompany me to the front door of my apartment building. I attributed my violent reaction to something in the salad, but after lying down a couple of hours I felt fine, and knew that the tension of my suppressed inner turmoil had caused the physical reaction.

"That same evening I listened to my tape two more times, and slowly things began to dawn on me. Intuitively I knew that I had heard the truth, that this truth was part of a universal principle, as was I, and that this impersonal, impartial principle

was not about to change for me, so I had better
make an effort to adjust my life to it. Subsequently
Frederick introduced me to the writings of Swami
Vivekananda, which he uses as the basis for his
lectures and which no thinking being will be able to
resist. Needless to say, my life has been greatly
changed."

Fritz at forty-two is somewhat older than most
of the outstanding young people who accept Frederick as their mentor, gathering at his homes in
New York and Massachusetts and soaking up his
philosophy. Since my Guides have identified these
as souls who knew Frederick as their leader on
Arcturus and some previous earth lives, I asked
each of them about themselves.

One of them is Elissa Melaragno, born in Provi-
dence, Rhode Island, in 1951, whose father is the
sculptor, Biagio P. Melaragno. After graduating
from St. Paul's, a Lutheran school, and attending
the University of Rhode Island, Elissa earned her
bachelor of fine arts degree at the University of
Georgia. During her twenties she taught art, man-
aged food cooperatives, developed community arts
projects, spent two years in Europe, and was married for five years to a Yale philosophy graduate.
She had also been seeking spiritual unfoldment,
and during her undergraduate days had "read every ancient scripture I could get my hands on. It
was the *Yoga Aphorisms of Patajali*, that ancient
Hindu text on Raja Yoga that changed my outlook.
Since then, although my disciplines of diet, study
and right-thinking were maintained, the prevailing
experience for me was one of being alone. Always
I would go on alone, seeking the next level of
initiation beyond groups, beyond relationships and

beyond my own limiting self-concepts, until I met Frederick and saw in him the embodiment of self-lessness and dedication to which I aspired.''

She had set up a painting studio in Northport, Long Island, when a friend told her of his chance reunion with Frederick, an old chum he had not seen in seven years, and of how greatly he had changed. Immediately she knew that she ''had to meet this spiritual person,'' and an appointment was arranged.

Elissa says of the encounter: ''As I entered the lobby of his Sutton Place apartment building, went up in the elevator and approached his door, I became increasingly aware that Frederick Von Mierers was more than just another astrologer. The feeling I experienced was one of immense tranquility in the midst of extraordinarily high radiation. He opened the door, and I was struck by his still, and calm yet piercing blue eyes, his perfectly refined Egyptian face, looking like a golden mask of Tutankhamen, and his tall statuesque physique.

''This same balance and perfection was reflected in his mirrored apartment, with its blue-violet lacquered walls. I felt comfortable and welcomed. Standing before the ancient Buddha, which was nestled amid lush plant life of azaleas, orchids and lilies, I realized that there were symbols present of every great world religion. Beyond the relaxing sounds of Kitaro's music I heard the gentle hum of negative ion machines and air purifiers. The city existed somewhere outside, but in here it was a sanctuary, a temple for the devoted and weary. My body revitalized cell by cell. At once I knew that I was embarking on the next stage of this soul's evolution. Frederick and I talked for hours about the impersonal, impartial Vedantic view. He would answer my specific questions before I had the chance to ask, and would tell me which lessons I would learn with him, and each was what I previously knew that I needed. Meeting Frederick confirmed for me, as it does for many others, that my level of dedication to my own God-self, therefore selfless service, was being acknowledged by the universe, and great progress was imminent."

Shortly afterwards she met John Andreadis, and they and a number of other students spent the summer at the Nantucket house where she "continually saw the example of Frederick's dedication to serving others, and in John witnessed living proof of the results of Frederick's contribution to the lives of others, because he takes his students to the realization that they are beyond all names and forms; that they can be perfect examples in mind, body and soul in the everyday world of God's perfection."

Since then Elissa has taken charge of the smooth running of Frederick's overflowing household, while he works with children and adults of all races and social classes, and she assists with the young women who come from the universities, including Harvard, Princeton and Yale.

"Within the New York City apartment and the large loft in which others live and work," she says, "Frederick accepts visitors from all over the world. He is interested in developing generals who are willing to help others, and not in establishing 'sick dependencies.' We use Vivekananda's *The Yogas and Other Works*, the Gospel of Sri Ramakrishna and the Old and New Testaments in the classes. These outline by comparison the work of Lords

Jesus, Rama and Krishna who were all immaculate
conceptions, all performed the same miracles and
were all incarnations of the Christ Consciousness
in physical form, incarnating at the exact point in
time and space necessary for the nations and races
of that time. These teachings have deepened my
own Judeo-Christian background to such a degree
that I feel at one with all of the great religions,
which is the essence of Frederick's teachings.

"I love the work that I am now doing. When
Frederick is in other parts of the country I and the
others manage everything: maintaining the apartment oasis, answering the calls, the requests for
lectures and tapes, and responses to the videos
shown all over the country, and helping each other
to grow. Except during the three summer months
we prepare a dinner for from thirty to sixty people
every Wednesday night, show Frederick's videos
and entertain guests who range from rabbis and
priests to actors and models, and from scientists
and business people to representatives of the media. Often I will cook and give lessons on diet.
Then Frederick and John will be surrounded by
people listening to their philosophy, and afterwards
perhaps we will all go dancing. It is a fabulous
life!"

Elissa felt that she might have undergone a "transition" while in Glastonbury, England, seven years
ago, but when I asked the Guides if she is a Walk-in,
they replied: "She did not come in as a new soul at
that time, but events occurred there that caused
her to realize her mission and to feel that she was a
stranger in the earth. Not until she met Frederick
several years later did she awaken to the real home,
her soul's home. Arcturus was the home for all of

those who are closely associated with Frederick, and they gravitated together here after Frederick, the original leader of them all, came into flesh as a Walk-in. Elissa was with them in several of their previous lifetimes on earth, including one when she was a high priestess in ancient Greece. John Hoyt was in ancient Egypt with Frederick and John at the time of the priestly temple ceremonies, and also of course on Arcturus.''

John Richards Hoyt is an economics major at Princeton University, and was a valued member of its football team until a shoulder injury ended his sports career. Tall, blond and extremely handsome, he grew up in Berwyn, the fashionable Main Line community outside Philadelphia, and he says of his early youth: "I come from a very conservative, Waspy background where good manners, academic excellence and strong moral fiber were insisted upon. But I often felt isolated from the family, because I just didn't seem to view things from their perspective. My strong Christian upbringing had provided me with a solid moral foundation, but I intuitively felt that there was much being left out or ignored. Following the 'Hoyt mold' I was academically successful, but during high school I was also very athletic and social, and began spending most of my time with friends.

"It was about this time that I met Frederick on the beach at Nantucket. We sat and talked for at least a couple of hours about the Vedanta philosophy, and although much of it confused me, I was nonetheless intrigued. It was such a logical approach to life. It was as if I had within myself many of the ideas that Frederick presented, but had not allowed them to surface."

Throughout the remainder of the summer John saw Frederick frequently, becoming more receptive to his ideas, and after graduating *cum laude* from the Haverford School he spent a year studying the A-levels at Haileyburg College outside of London, England, where he was on his own for the first time, learning confidence in his own judgment. Returning to America he enrolled at Princeton, and spent his summers doing commercials, acting and modeling, while living in Frederick's New York apartment.

"My professional name is Hoyt Richards [the middle and last names reversed] and my success has been fortunate," he says, "but the true success story has been my increased spiritual awakening since I have been working with Frederick. He has taught me to make my own decisions in life, but always to be aware of the repercussions. He taught me to listen and observe myself in all situations, for it is only God experienced in another infinite realm of life. By helping me to become more conscious of my unconscious self Frederick showed me that you can see yourself in everyone. Individuality disappears. We are all waves in the ocean of life. Our world is in its present mess because of the prevalent feeling of separation from God. We must remember our original purpose on this planet, to see God and love Him. Frederick is devoting his life to this service, and I am honored to be able to serve and help."

Burkhard Hoene, another of the group who knew Frederick in ancient Egypt and on Arcturus, was born in 1957, the son of a doctor, and grew up in a happy, gregarious family in New Hampshire, where he and his four brothers and sisters "often had projects together, from building houses to working in the woods." In high school he was president of the student body and active in athletics, but after entering the University of Virginia, he says, "I developed an unusual drive to follow international affairs, and I originated an international business-living-learning program at the university. I later studied at the United Nations in Geneva, Switzerland." He is currently the youngest buyer ever employed by Brooks Brothers, that conservative citadel of gentlemen's apparel, where he designs and works with its manufacturers worldwide.

Burkhard recalls meeting Frederick and John several years ago "at a party given by a well-respected family in New York," and although he had escorted "a girl friend from Switzerland" to the party, he spent the entire evening "talking with Frederick about higher principles." He says that his life "changed quickly after that, as I studied with Frederick, who stressed a strict diet and the study of Vivekananda's works. He otherwise encouraged me as I passed through two years of performances, orchestrating evenings with young European, South American, Polynesian and Oriental girls in New York, and we had so much fun that several top nightclubs, including Studio 54, asked us to give parties there, at the clubs' expense. But all of this activity is merely a means to an end, because I want to be of service. Frederick would tell me that all I ever experienced was God. This is because you can't be where you are unless you've been where you've been. Without opposites there can be no comparisons, without comparisons no knowledge, without knowledge no realization, and without realization there can be no resurrection. I've been with Frederick two years now, assisting him wherever possible, and I feel privileged to be able to do so."

The tall, attractive charmer is planning to organize a worldwide group of young potential leaders representing all major international corporations, countries, religions, sciences and entertainment, handpicked by the leaders of those organizations and governments, "to create a bond among the world's influential young." He says that it will transcend all boundaries "and is for the purpose of knowledge, not power; for service, not special interests," because he feels that the young are more open-minded to service and idealistic goals if they feel that their efforts will have an effect.

Kristopher Pratt, another Arcturian, is the great-great-great-grandson of the inventer of the Colt .45 revolver and founder of the *Scientific American* magazine. Before Kristopher met Frederick he was training in track and field for the Olympics, while studying for a university degree in business. Six feet five inches tall, he had the requisite long legs, but knee injuries forced him to drop out of Olympics competition, and he was feeling empty and lost when he had a life reading with Frederick that changed the direction of his life. "The reading went to the depths of all the major events in my life, including family and personal relationships," he muses. "Frederick described these in a way that made it clear to me why these problems or assets were in my life, and what lessons I would learn from them. He also revealed my deep psychological behavior patterns and showed me how my thoughts created my life, and that I was the cause of my own destiny. My life reading was an experience that was simultaneously a shock, a revelation and a relief. There was no question. I knew that a new and more serious path was now before me, and that I had the basic tools of life specifically appropriate for myself."

"When I began studying under Frederick," he declared, "I was taken beyond all previous conceptions. The discipline was rigid. Many lessons came with a great degree of difficulty. All too often I would either overreact or become intensely frustrated, but always Frederick's words would resound. In innumerable ways I was shown exactly how the lack of attention to detail in my life was the cause of my every problem. Frederick knew exactly where the flaws in my character were, and the process known as creative conflict that he taught gave me the ability to see clearly just what my weaknesses were and how to overcome them. This was done with impersonal and impartial care on Frederick's part, and never once did he impose his will on me."

Kristopher says that Frederick trained him to become an interior painter, introduced him to famed decorator Billy Baldwin, and helped him to launch a highly successful career as a painting contractor. During those years Frederick appeared on a popular call-in radio program nightly, on which he discussed science and religion. Kristopher recalls: "Frederick found poor children who came to him through his radio show that covered all of Long Island, New York City and Westchester, and I have since worked with a host of these young people who are dedicated to this work. It provides a learning tool for them, so that they can discover these same wonderful lessons of life while simultaneously studying with Frederick. I am now one of New York City's leading painting contractors for the top interior decorators. We work in all the exclusive areas of New York, Southampton and Nantucket, and we make walls look like lacquer, marble, lapis lazuli, and employ all the special glazing finishes, such as stippling, as well as creating murals and trompe l'oeil effects.

"I have known Frederick for nine years, but have observed remarkable changes in him since 1978 [when he became a Walk-in from Arcturus]. He suddenly developed the ability to see the deep inner character of people within minutes of meeting them, down to the depths of their souls. It was and is astounding to me. He had me study Vivekananda's works, which is the textbook he uses and which covers the entire scope of metaphysical philosophy. It answers all the questions that one may have, for it is a devastatingly impersonal and impartial analysis of every behavioral pattern in humanity. One cannot squeeze out of anything through laziness and self-indulgence, and the book unifies science, philosophy and religion down to the last molecule."

Errol Legh Erener, an air force second lieutenant who has a degree in physics and hopes to become an astronaut, was drawn to Frederick after hearing him on a radio show. "To this day I cannot explain why, but I had an irresistible urge to call him for an astrological reading," he recalls, "and when I did so he began telling me things about myself that no one except I knew. About a week later I met him at his apartment, to hear his astrological tape about me, and it told my whole life story down to the last niche. I was astounded by the enormity of it all. The first thing that impressed me about Frederick was that he was not interested in fulfilling his own ego. What he teaches is for everyone, and the very nature of the material he introduces emphasizes impartiality as the way to God. Since meeting him my life has been changed from that of a very shy and self-doubting individual to one who can stand on his own two feet. What has most amazed me about the Vedanta teachings to which Frederick introduced me is that it totally blows away any feeble scientific attempt to undermine God's place in the universe. Not only this, but my own studies in physics have shown me that there is a profound connection between science and metaphysics.

"Everything that I have learned through Frederick has inspired me to put away my selfish desires and to live my life in service to God. This doesn't mean that I am not going to continue to try to become an astronaut. I strongly believe in my country, and we need to have warriors ready to defend our nation's security. That is why I joined the air force. What it does mean is that I have attempted to depersonalize this goal, so that I am doing this to serve God by being an example to others."

Audrey Isakson, after graduating from Douglass College, went into the field of social work to help battered children. In the fall of 1983 she met John Andreadis in her capacity as coordinator of the New York Whole Life Expo, an exposition having to do with holistic approaches to health and well-being from the personal to the planetary level. One of her tasks was to assemble information on videotapes to be shown at the Expo, and John dropped by regarding the video tapes called "The Eternal

Values" that Frederick provides free to cable TV and local television stations in San Diego, Los Angeles, Boston, San Francisco, Westchester, New York and elsewhere. Through John she met Frederick, and she says of him: "Frederick's insights into my past, the beauty and serenity of the environment he has created, the strength of his presence all made an indelible impression on my consciousness." She began to adopt the dietary practices that he recommended for her, while studying Vivekananda's books, and she praises Frederick and John "for my deepening experience of surrender to God and an attendant lessening of the hold on my ego."

Catherine Edelmann, a senior at Princeton University, met Frederick during her junior year through John Hoyt, a classmate she had known for two years. "John had spent the past summer under Frederick's guidance," she explains, "and that fall I noticed an extraordinary transformation in John's character. He was suddenly more accessible and receptive to others' ideas, and there was a newly revealed light in his eyes. He was glowing. After many discussions, John took me to meet Frederick and I spent a day and evening in his apartment—a violet world overflowing with plants, strains of Kitaro's music, and highly energized individuals discussing God. I emerged changed for life. I had been unclear for many years as to my concept of God, but after watching Frederick's video tapes I came away with the conviction of God's absolute existence.

"My world has since expanded enormously through the guidance of Vivekananda's books. I have come to know the oneness of my mind with God's mind, and to know that the power of His thought is the power of my thought. I have brought things to happen by calling on the forces of the infinite I AM which is within me. For example, last spring I applied for an internship with a high-ranking United States senator in Washington, D.C. The odds were horrendously unfavorable because hundreds of students apply for this prestigious internship, with only fourteen available spots. I had the qualifications, but no political connections, nor am I a politics major interested in a political career, but I declared every day that I would get it, keeping faith with the Infinite Self which is the I AM of everyone, and I was selected."

An English major, Catherine says that her ability to understand and write her thesis on Ralph Waldo Emerson was the result of Frederick's teaching, and she adds: "I am awed by all that he has come to teach. I intend, with his guidance, to determine my mission in life, and to fulfill it with absolute faith in the love and power of God."

My Guides have written of Glenn Dove, another member of Frederick's group: "He was prominent in the days of Aristotle, when he was a counselor to the court, and recalls much ancient wisdom from that period, as well as from Arcturus." At the age of four Glenn had a minor operation, and while recuperating at home was awakened during the night by a man who was standing in the corner of his room. The next day he described the man to his mother, relating what the man had told him, but he had no idea of the man's identity until someone sent his mother a picture of Jesus, and the little boy exclaimed, "That's the man I saw in my room."

Thereafter he began to see auras around people and to receive visitations from his grandfather, who had recently died. In his teens he started reading books on religion, meditation and the higher teachings, and in his early twenties was well launched in a musical career when, driving home one night from a recording session, he happened to tune in the car radio to the Joel Martin show.

"Frederick was speaking," he remembers, "and he was the first person to put together all the ideals that I believed in. I couldn't get that station on my home radio, so I sat in the driveway for the next half hour to hear the rest of it. Through the radio show, I contacted Frederick and had a life reading, in which he told me that I had psychic abilities but had misused them in past lives and must now be very careful of them. Even before this was brought to my attention, the most important thing to me was following the path of God. I now give a limited number of readings each week, trying to offer the guidance that will help others grow toward their own inner self-realization and union with God."

Several years ago Glenn received a late-night telephone call from John Andreadis, asking for a reading "that couldn't wait until morning." Of that curious call, he says: "In my usual readings I pick up loved ones that have passed on, but to my surprise the ones who came in for John were from other planets or star systems. They said John had very important work that was about to begin and would truly change the course of events. In a previous reading I had told John that he would soon meet a twin of his who came from another part of the globe and would be doing the same work that John was doing. Shortly thereafter he met Nicolas Chrissakis from Greece, and their friendship has developed as I said that it would. After reading *Strangers Among Us* I knew that I would contribute to helping people through the shift of the earth

on its axis, and although the discipline seemed
quite difficult, I decided to work with Frederick
and John and their group. Since I am twenty-nine
years old, I expect to be around at the end of this
century when the shift occurs.''

The other member of Frederick's inner circle is
Gerald Nissman, a New York importer of precious
jewels who was commissioned in 1967 to go to
Russia to appraise a fabulous collection of emeralds. Nissman was sought out by Frederick in 1980,
and he says of the encounter: "Frederick said that
he had been searching for an honest, ethical gem
dealer and after meditating on it came to the conviction that I was the one. He bought a fortune in
gems for himself, thirteen stones, which he said
had to be identical to those in the breastplate worn
by Moses and other high priests of all major religions. These included diamonds, emeralds, rubies,
cat's eyes, an uncultured pearl, and an imperial
precious topaz. All had to be of a specific size.
Then he began to send me his students, those
closest to him for whom he had prescribed their
proper gems. Thus started my relationship with
Frederick, who said that I had been with him in
past incarnations in Egypt, India and Atlantis and
had prepared the stones for him there as well."

Nissman and his family are Jewish, but he says
that the study of the Yogas recommended by Frederick has enriched their lives. "I believe what Frederick says, that Vedanta is the religion of the entire
universe, all the way up beyond the galactic center," he declares. "Our relationship with Frederick has rekindled my family's belief in one God
and life beyond physical death. As he explains it,
the elements of the body are atomic vibration, as
are the elements of the gems. The gem whose

atomic vibration is in harmony with, or supplements the deficiency in one's electromagnetic thought field is prescribed, and when our energy fields are supplemented, then our entire vibrational field, or thought field is put into balance. However, the gems balance us on a higher vibrational level and thus enable us to perceive the subtler creative energies of the universe and tune in to higher vibrational thoughts and ideas. Frederick has also described how this vibrational harmonizing enables us to tune in to the thoughts of space people. He says that this works much in the same way as fine-tuning a radio, because everything is electromagnetic energy on this particular level in this system."

These, then, are the Arcturians closest to Frederick, and when I asked the Guides to comment on them as a group they wrote: "They all came from Arcturus through the normal birth process in order to help humankind as the shift of the earth on its axis approaches, and this event will mark the end of the Piscean Age and the dawn of the New Age. Their vibrations are of the highest order, and each knew Frederick in previous earthly lives. Some are more highly developed than others, but all are so far above ordinary mortals in their perceptions and spirituality that they are to be highly regarded. Catherine will develop into a counselor and leader, as will Hoene. Erener will become a recognized leader in the New Order, and Nissman is a good and honest merchant who has dealt with gems in many lifetimes and would not knowingly take advantage of anyone. As for the importance of gems, they do indeed lift the consciousness and open the mind to insight beyond the usual human realm. Go ahead and get them, Ruth. They are important."

Well, I guess the Guides have finally talked me
into it. I have been aware for many years, of course,
that famed psychic Edgar Cayce also emphasized
the importance of gems, and often prescribed certain ones for those for whom he gave life readings.
He too spoke of the breastplates of Moses and the
high priests, and of the symbology and importance
of the jewels embedded there. These gems are not
for flaunting, but as in the case of Frederick and
his group, are to be worn at all times touching the
skin, usually beneath the clothing. Both Cayce and
Frederick have stressed that the gems, to be effective, must weigh two to three carats each and be as
nearly flawless as possible. Unfortunately, they
are expensive, and I am told that the effect can be
harmful if we wear gems that clash with our own
atomic attunement.

In fact, a booklet issued by Edgar Cayce headquarters states: "Just as it is desirable for us to be
aware of the different uses to which atomic energy
can be put, so is it well for us to realize that there
are destructive, as well as constructive uses for
gems, stones and metals." But it also quotes
Paramahansa Yogananda as advising: "Pearls and
other jewels as well as metals and plants, applied
directly to the human skin, exercise an electromagnetic influence over the physical cells. Man's body
contains carbon and various metallic elements that
are present also in plants, metals and jewels. The
discoveries of the rishis in these fields will doubt-
less receive confirmation someday from physiolo-
gists. Man's sensitive body, with its electrical life
currents, is a center of many mysteries as yet
unexplored."

Yogananda recalled the words of his own Master, Sri Yukteswar: "Just as a house may be fitted

CHAPTER TEN

Mission to Maui

INHABITANTS of Maui, that idyllic island in America's Hawaiian chain, may not know it, but according to psychic sources they are living in one of the earth's most powerful vibratory centers for contacting space beings. And hopefully, this power source is soon to be harnessed to awaken our higher consciousness.

Björn Örtenheim, the Swedish scientist-inventor whom I introduced in my previous book *Threshold to Tomorrow* plans to move his base of operations from Sweden to Maui because he believes he has discovered there a tremendous vibration that can link him more closely to Power of Light, as he calls his guiding-spirit source, and thereby uplift humanity.

Björn has been told by Power of Light that the

capital city and scientific center of the lost continent of Lemuria, that legendary landmass in the Pacific Ocean, was located just off the coast of Maui, and that its positive vibrations can be utilized by means of a powerful crystal that he possesses, to open new horizons for mankind.

Readers of *Threshold to Tomorrow* are aware that my Guides, as well as the highly evolved Walk-in whom I call Michael, separately identified Björn to me as the Walk-in soul of Albert Einstein, that towering intellect whose advances in the realm of scientific thought helped to revolutionize our understanding of the cosmos. The transferral of egos was said to have occurred during a hypnotic sleep on a beach in western Sweden during a howling windstorm in 1967. Björn, a discouraged, deeply unhappy man of thirty-six, had taken with him a shotgun which he intended to use to end his life, but during that comalike sleep a substitution of egos apparently occurred, and he awakened with electrifying new goals and scientific talents.

Soon thereafter he became aware that during sleep he was being instructed by a group of otherworld entities who were telling him how to develop clean energy sources and to perfect inventions that could raise the consciousness of humankind. In answer to my questions about this phenomenon, my own Guides wrote: "The soul of Einstein lives now in Björn's body. He is in direct contact with highly developed soul sources in the galaxy, and because of his performances in past lives he is given every assistance to speed the rediscovery of forms of energy that will revolutionize the world in the twenty-first century."

A strong leader soon emerged within the spirit group that was directing Björn's work, and in early

1981 Björn said that he appeared to him in a waking vision, identifying himself simply as Power of Light. At Björn's request I asked the Guides for further identification of this strong spirit, and they replied that another name for him was "Seraphim, or Serapis, an archangel directing the force of light transformed from darkness," and that he had wielded great influence on many Europeans, including Johann Sebastian Bach and Franz Liszt.

Shortly before Björn's vision, he and his wife, Angela, had visited me in Washington, D.C., enroute to California, and while on the West Coast he seemed unable to achieve a clear contact with Power of Light, whom he had begun to call POL. On returning to Sweden the channels were again open, and while proceeding with his clean energy projects he also received important scientific assignments from the Swedish government and academics, as well as from the United Nations. Meanwhile POL had begun instructing him how to build a pyramid and use a powerful crystal to open the awareness of human beings, and on a subsequent trip to Maui in 1983 Björn discovered a power center that seemed made to order for this important undertaking.

POL, in commenting on the trip, told him, "I led you to the bottom half of the ancient pyramid of Lemuria at Maui. It is a very interesting building since it is over 50,000 years old by earth time. You also visited the sacred temple where a light ray was striking you despite the inclement weather. Now I am going to give you the exact position of the capital city of Lemuria, which is under water in the bay just outside of Maui. This city was named Denerali, and many parts of it are still intact. It may be possible to dive there and vacuum away some of the covering sand, so that you will find the remains of buildings. The scientific center containing a large crystal [similar to the one on Atlantis] is still there beneath the waters. I recommend that you make a floating platform and anchor it directly above the crystal. Then with your amplifier and your crystal, using the black hole and the lenses, you can create a tremendously powerful magnetic power field where people can experience the energies and the amplified Universal Magnetic Field, UMF, created by the contact between your crystal and the crystal of Lemuria on the ocean floor.

"Individuals will have varying experiences relevant to their own vibrational level, because there are almost as many vibrational levels as there are people. Some will see into the future and have visions. Some will see situations in their past lives. Others will be reinforced with the strength and power to reach their goal, if the goal is on the side of Light and not of Darkness. People with very low vibrations will probably feel tired, because their subconscious will fight the rising consciousness and a kind of interior blockage may occur. I suggest that you ask everyone to write down his reactions. The experience is absolutely harmless, because these energies are on such a high frequency that they cannot affect any organic tissues, or anything in the physical body except the vibrations."

POL then gave Björn specific directions for situating the platform above the Lemurian crystal, but told him to divulge this location to no one until he was ready to erect the platform. In discussing his new project, Björn confided, "POL has been telling me for some time to concentrate on raising the consciousness of people all over the world, and to teach them how to increase their brain capacity by using harmonies from light, colors and sound at the same time that they are resting in the stabilizing vibrations from the amplified UMF. Although I shall continue to work on the hydrogen clean-energy projects that the Dark Forces are trying to block, I am now concentrating on the move to Maui, to build POL's Center for Higher Consciousness and an amplifier system for giving people the opportunity to increase their brain capacity in the UMF.''

Before discovering the strong vibrations on Maui, Björn and Angela had first visited Ceylon, which according to the former "has one of the strongest focus points on the whole earth. The reason that it was chosen as a focus point in the beginning was because it has a naturally formed pyramid higher than any man-made pyramid in the world. Due to this, the leaders of Lemuria were hiding their sacred scrolls of universal wisdom in a cave of that pyramid before Lemuria sank into the sea, and the scrolls are still there after 50,000 years, as is the power field. That is why so many people from all religions are attracted to the place without quite knowing why.''

Björn quotes POL as telling him: "The original Singalese people were remnants of the Lemurian society. The strong vibration of the great natural pyramid and the secret of universal wisdom and scientific knowledge that are kept in the focal point of the cave within the pyramid are a key to how these people could have remained in peace and harmony with nature for many thousands of years.''

My Guides have frequently declared that the Lemurians were peaceable, loving, spiritually advanced people, in contrast to the more warlike, technologically developed Atlanteans with whom they shared the leadership of the prehistoric world.

POL apparently agreed with Björn after his Hawaiian visit that Maui would be a better selection than Ceylon for launching his Center for Higher Consciousness, perhaps because the leadership of world affairs is currently centered in the Western world. I asked Björn to query POL about this choice, since I am not in contact with that spiritual being, and he sent me a copy of the message that came through: "My Brother, this is the answer to Ruth's questions about Maui. At that island are located the remains of three philosophical and scientific centers. You have visited two of them: the remains of the pyramid of which the Polynesian inhabitants of the island were long unaware and the place of philosophical meditation where you rested in the sun-ray. There is another such place in a cave that you will discover later. Maui was the center of science and philosophy on Lemuria, and when the shift of the earth on its axis occurs at the end of this century, parts of the continent of Lemuria will rise several thousand feet from the ocean bottom, as will Maui.

"The reason why we are interested in focusing our energies there is because we want to recall to earthlings the humanistic and philosophical vibrations of the Lemurian society once centered there. This can be of great assistance to you in the consciousness-raising concept, but you must be on guard against those people who work for the Powers of Darkness under a pretended Power of Light."

Björn describes Maui as the Mother Center, the heart chakra of the earth, adding: "Maui is therefore the feminine principle of the earth, as opposed to the Mediterranean-Atlantic area which is the masculine principle, and it is where the love vibration can be most enhanced. The different islands in the state of Hawaii are from very different origins and ages. Maui is more than four hundred million years old, according to geological findings. The black granite rocks on Maui are the same as those in Scandinavia, whereas the big island, Hawaii, is only around fifty thousand years old and consists mainly of volcanic lava and gravel.''

I asked Björn to explain more fully the role of Power of Light, and he replied that POL is ''in charge of the ultimate energy and source of life in our universe, the Universal Magnetic Field, UMF.'' He insists that POL is not to be thought of as a person, but as one of the highest servants of the Creator, and that he has instructed Björn how to build a resonance amplifier of the UMF, ''using the pace of the earth's magnetic field in combination with light, sounds and magnetic pulses to amplify all the vibrations in the UMF and feed them in a harmonic tuning into human life vibrations.'' He says that when this is constructed people can ''rest in harmony and increase their brain capacity simply by absorbing the right vibrations in the UMF. These vibrations will also strengthen physical power, and release people from disturbing tensions and other effects in their bodies and brains that make it difficult for them to reach their positive goals.''

On Maui, Björn hopes also to establish an American Center of Cosmic Science, ''where for the first time in our modern age we can really open the door between the natural and supernatural based on real science. Extraterrestrial contract and communication with higher intelligences of other universes will be possible for this group of selected people.''

I asked Björn why there are fewer sightings of UFOs now than in recent decades, and he showed me a current Swedish newspaper featuring a picture of a large space vehicle, saying, "There have been several sightings over Scandinavia recently. This newspaper photograph has been tested by photographic and military experts, using an electron microscope, and they say that there is no indication of forgery. It [the UFO] was also spotted by the military radar."

Björn quoted Power of Light as saying, "The large space fleets in your solar system are protected from being seen from earth by a special magnetic shield that makes them invisible to radar, cameras and the naked eye. The ship that was seen in the newspaper picture was outside of this protective field because it had made a landing in the mountainous area of Norway. That's why it could be photographed just after takeoff. Later, when it had accelerated to its normal speed it could not be photographed by a conventional camera."

Apparently in the decades of the 1950s and 1960s, when so many UFO sightings were reported that the United States government felt compelled to launch an investigation through Operation Blue Book, the space travelers had felt no fear of being observed while they observed us. They were said to be on friendly missions, and they seemingly made numerous landings to investigate soil, animals, vegetation and even humans at close range. But some of the UFOs were reportedly shot down by armed aircraft, and subsequently our space friends seem to have become more cautious about materializing both themselves and their craft.

Several years ago Björn sent me a color slide of a UFO which he personally snapped while piloting a Super Cub along the west coast of Sweden near Copenhagen. "I was flying at about 3,000 feet," he recalls, "when suddenly this strange craft appeared beside me. I began doing acrobatics, trying to prevent a close encounter, but the UFO followed my maneuvers perfectly. I then grabbed my camera and took pictures of it, while it followed me for ten minutes, but suddenly it accelerated far more rapidly than a normal craft could do, and disappeared abruptly from my view."

Björn quotes POL as saying that there are many civilizations similar to ours on other planets, but most are millions of years older and much more highly developed. "If you reduce the life span of earth to twenty-four hours," he continued, "man would have existed there for less than twenty seconds, and in the last second he has brought his world to the brink of extinction by ignoring the words of the Creator and the codes of His perfect creation, your undisturbed Nature." POL further told Björn that most of the UFOs now being observed on earth are remote-controlled, "collecting tests and making temperature measurements from your atmosphere in order to control the conditions of your environment. Some 50,000 years ago a nuclear war occurred on earth, but because there were fewer destructive weapons then it was minor compared to what could occur today. So many people were killed and so much destruction occurred that the survivors had to hide most of their lives in caves and other remote places until the environment could again be hospitable for life. Those survivors had to start again from the very beginning, without books and technical equipment, since most of the learned ones were killed during the war, or died shortly thereafter from radiation."

POL says that numerous space people from other planets are now entering the earthly sphere as Walk-

ins, to help with the decontamination and to uplift
our consciousness, while most of the space vehicles are unmanned, remote-controlled capsules for
testing our environment. He reportedly told Björn:
''Ruth's question about how to dematerialize spacecraft and move them faster in the universe is easy.
Everything is energy. Different forms of matter are
different forms of energy, with different frequencies holding the atoms, molecules and electrons
together. By changing the frequency and the form
of energy you can disassemble the pattern of this
matter and turn it into energy. Energy can be immediately transported from one place to another
through the UMF. To reassemble complicated patterns of matter like a spacecraft is impossible for
human beings, but not for highly developed entities
in other galaxies. It is possible to move spacecraft
from one place in the universe to another by changing the frequencies in the UMF. My group and I
are not traveling on spacecraft. We are from a
totally different dimension and are only existing in
spirit form as divine consciousness energy. We can
appear and be seen by the entities and people who
work for us when it is necessary, but not by others.''

Inasmuch as my Guides have for several years
been telling me that highly developed space people
have mastered the ability to project themselves
and their space vehicles from other dimensions
into earth's atmosphere by disassembling and reassembling the atoms, I could accept POL's explanation. After all, it is also beyond my comprehension
to understand how television pictures are projected
through the ether and almost instantly reassembled
on my TV screen. It would seem only one giant
step forward for more advanced beings—our space

friends—to project themselves and their UFOs into our skies.

POL says of this alleged accomplishment: "No forms of organic life can travel in space at a speed exceeding the speed of light. When matter or organic life forms approach the speed of light they are converted into another form of energy called plasma, and their identity form is separated into the smallest microcosms, nuclear molecules. At that time they become an energy part of UMF. Since the UMF also contains the divine information on how to reassemble all these energy forms into all kinds of matter and organic life, it is possible to create life and matter anywhere in the universe where there is a possibility for these forms to sustain their identity. Highly developed souls are a very complex form of divine energy and consciousness. They also contain the energy of creativity, which is a direct vibration from the power of the Creator. Thus, a soul cannot be divided into plasma parts and be reassembled because the soul is from a different dimension where there is no matter or organic life, but a soul can be directed as a divine form of ultimate energy by an entity in a higher dimension.

"You may wonder if it is possible to transport disassembled organic life forms in plasma form through the universe over distances that would not be possible for the organic life form, because of the aging process of the organic cells during the long period that would occur if traveling slower than the speed of light. For instance, the distance from your planet to the closest one with suitable life conditions would take more than 10 million light-years, traveling at a speed of 99 percent of the speed of light. Yes, organic life has to age, but not necessarily as fast as it does on your planet."

In May of 1981 Björn wrote to tell me that he had "suddenly remembered" a place that he has visited several times between lives. He described a planet composed of rolling hills, between which are fjords linked in a labyrinth of continuous light-green waters. "Light-green grass covers the hillsides, and everywhere are small bushes with flowers of fantastic colors and beautiful aroma," he declared. "There are no large animals, but birds in all colors of the rainbow. The atmosphere is like a moving light cloud that is continuously changing colors from pink to blue. The days are shorter, and one rests about three to four hours. The people weigh much less than here on earth, although their appearance is similar to ours. When they walk they barely touch the ground, and are dressed in long light-colored robes. The temperature is constant at all times, because the sun is a quasar and is filtered by those clouds that are covering the entire planet in numerous layers. If this atmosphere were to disappear you could be hit by a ray from the quasar sun that would burn you to ashes within seconds.

"No one eats solid foods there. You get all the energy from the quasar sun and from drinking a liquid made from the flowers: light yellow in the morning and dark green before the evening rest period. I have never seen any aggression or disease there, no hard work, machinery, or any mechanized thing, and it's like a resting place for spirits where you can recharge your consciousness with knowledge fed to your soul directly through the extremely intense Universal Magnetic Field that contains all information on the progress of life."

Continuing his description of the planet, Björn

said: "I remember an incident the first time I was there. I went up to a colorful bush and tried to pet it with my hand, because it was so beautiful, and I received an enormous electric shock, with colorful sparks flying all around me. Everybody laughed in a friendly way and helped me up, since I had fallen on my backside, and one of them said, 'We thought you, who knew so much about energy, would recognize a power plant.' The place is called Theohim, and it's a kind of university of highest cosmic vibrational consciousness where you are fed with knowledge from the extremely intense UMF. The intensity is much stronger than on earth because of the nearness of the planet to the quasar sun and the vibrations of the powers of light. One has no conception of time there. You find some interesting personality and have a discussion with him that seems like several days, and suddenly he is gone. But new personalities appear, and there is never any consideration of time. You could be there a week, a year, or a hundred years and you'd never know the difference."

This description sounded like a pleasant fantasy to me at the time that Björn first typed out his recollection of the "memory." But when I later met Frederick Von Mierers and others who were said to have entered earth life directly from other planets, it began to have a familiar ring. I therefore asked the Guides if they could identify the planet where Björn had previously sojourned, and they replied: "Björn is remembering Arcturus, where he knew Frederick and the others in his group. The area that he visited in that vision is known as Theohim, but it is a part of Arcturus and his description is basically correct. He was there both before and after he entered the earth life as Albert

Einstein. However, it was beyond Andromeda where he visited immediately before reentry this time, to prepare himself for overcoming the Dark Forces here, since on Arcturus all is light and goodness, and he would otherwise have been ill-equipped for coping here in this important mission."

Frederick, who was unaware of this comment by my Guides, told me as soon as we met, "Ruth, I must get in touch with Björn Örtenheim. I knew him on Arcturus, and it is essential that I help to bring his vitally important work to fruition before the shift."

The meeting was arranged late in 1984 when Björn, Angela and their two-year-old son Mikael stopped to see me in Washington, D.C., enroute to Maui for their new beginning. Björn brought with him two large, dazzling crystals of pyramidal contour, one to be used in meditation and the other to surmount the platform above the Lemurian crystal that POL says is in the bay off Maui.

During his visit Björn recounted a dramatic incident in which he says that Angela's life was saved by Power of Light. His story is this: During a trip to Los Angeles four years ago his wife underwent toxic shock from wearing a tampon, became unconscious, and was "gasping in death throes." Frantic, Björn dashed to the lobby of the building where they had rented an apartment without individual telephones, and called a doctor who grumpily told him to give her an aspirin. It was three o'clock in the morning. "I pounded on an apartment door through which I could hear loud rock music," he recalls, "but they would not open the door, and we were strangers there. I rushed back upstairs, opened our door and beheld a brilliant shaft of light coming down over the bed where Angela lay. Then, in the shimmering light I saw POL in white and gold costume holding his hands above her. He looked at me, and I felt total harmony. She began breathing normally, her fever vanished, as did POL, and she hasn't been sick since.''

POL apparently had work for Angela to do, because on their return to Sweden he began giving Björn instructions for a book on survival that he wanted her to write. Angela, who is of Creole and American Indian extraction, protested that she had no writing talents and lacked the experience or education to produce such a technical book. "But POL told her that she would have all the help that she needed from his 'Sister of Light,' " Björn says. "He told her simply to start writing about survival. She did, and suddenly all kinds of Swedish scientists, professors and survival experts appeared and helped her to get the correct information. The material fell into place, and a Swedish publisher will soon be bringing it out in English."

The title of her book is *To Survive or Not to Survive,* and it deals with the crucial problems that will face humankind if a world war or natural catastrophe occurs. These run the gamut from how to make fires and proper shelter, to finding water; protecting oneself from lightning or nuclear radiation; camping, hunting and fishing techniques; selecting edible plants and herbs to maintain life; and collecting survival equipment that should be amassed and stored. Stig Lundquist, professor of atmospheric electricity at Uppsala University in Sweden, and according to Björn a member of the Royal Academy that helps select Nobel Prize winners, has written a highly complimentary introduction to Angela's book, calling it insightful and beneficial.

POL agrees with my Guides that World War III

can be averted, particularly if we maintain peace
through August of 1986. But both our sources de-
clare that the shift of the earth on its axis at the
close of this century is inevitable, and is a necessary cleansing process for the world that we have
sadly abused through pollution and evildoing. In
either event it is of paramount importance for those
who wish to continue in physical body to learn
survival techniques.

Angela says that she has had no direct contact
with POL, and must communicate with him solely
through Björn. But curiously, during recent months
several other Arcturians besides Björn are convinced that they have experienced his presence.
Frederick Von Mierers recently disclosed that he
had a direct vision of him this past summer, but at
the time did not realize his identity. Then John
Andreadis, while speaking with Björn on transatlantic telephone shortly before their meeting this
fall, was told that "the three of you in your room
just now should meditate as soon as we get off the
phone, because POL has a surprise for you."

John says of the strange encounter: "There was
no normal way that Björn could have known how
many of us were in the room, but immediately
upon ending the conversation the three of us sat in
triangular formation, held hands and began meditation. Shortly thereafter all of us had experiences of
tremendous force and color, with the pure, undu-
lated rays of the UMF cleaning our auras. The
next day I called Björn in Sweden to tell him of our
mutual experience, and he said that is exactly what
happens when POL comes. He added that sometimes POL appears in a form that looks like a man,
and at that moment I had a vision of POL's form. I
put it down to imagination, but during the next two

days the same form kept appearing to me, and at last I went to Frederick to describe what I saw. Halfway into my description he interrupted me, and continued it himself. Everything that he described about the form he had seen last summer, but never mentioned to me, was identical to my vision, even down to the color, type and amount of clothing that the man wore. After we met Björn, he said that we were describing exactly how POL appears to him.''

John says that many of Frederick's students describe experiences of seeing POL's radiance during meditation, and feeling his power. ''I know that anyone who is sincere and will work for the Light in the coming years will be able to feel his presence and gain his support,'' he said. ''It is therefore better not to describe his exact appearance now, because we do not want others to have preconceived notions of what they may see. POL is not here to be worshiped, but to help us attune to the Creator. The only true power is God. Power of Light is his messenger, as are others. He will help us, but *we* must do the work.''

Sometimes small, seemingly unimportant incidents occur that are more convincing than the broad sweep of events. I should therefore like to recount two interesting sidelights, as follows.

Because I had informed Frederick this fall of the Örtenheims' arrival time at Kennedy International Airport in New York, where they would be changing planes for their onward flight to my home in Washington, he met their plane with a large delegation of well-wishers. Neither he nor Björn had seen a picture of the other, or heard a description, but there was instant recognition despite the surge of humanity in that teeming terminal. I was told by others that Frederick was simply one of twenty in the welcoming group, and was standing well back, so I asked Björn how he could instantly have picked him out in the crowd.

"Because he looks just like Power of Light," Björn replied. "He is not POL, of course, but had he been dressed in those white garments I could have thought that I was seeing a vision. The likeness is astonishing."

Later I asked Frederick how he had recognized Björn among the hundreds of travel-worn passengers emerging from the huge transatlantic jet, and he said simply, "I knew him from Arcturus."

The other intriguing incident occurred the next day at my home. Björn was expressing his pleasure at the overwhelmingly favorable reaction among scientists and the academic world to my chapter about him in *Threshold to Tomorrow*, when he interrupted his report to remark, "Ruth, Power of Light had told me I could trust you, because you have Norwegian blood."

My mouth literally fell open as I stared back at him. I am of German and English stock, and not until recently, during genealogical research at the Library of Congress, did I stumble across the fact that my earliest known American ancestor was a Norseman, born in Fredrikstad in 1607, who arrived in the New World only sixteen years after the Mayflower landed at Plymouth Rock. Since no relative had been aware of this information, and nothing about my link with the Norseman had ever been published or discussed outside my immediate family, how could Björn have known this?

Stumbling over my words, I blurted out the name of the wrong ancestor (which is easy to do when

thirteen generations have been researched at once),
but Björn responded, "No, POL told me the name
was Bratt."

I rushed to check my research, which was tucked
away on a closet shelf, and promptly verified that
the name of my first American progenitor was Albert Andriessen Bratt (Bradt), a Norwegian who
set sail with his family from Texel, Holland, September 25, 1636, on the ship *Rensselaerswyck*. Because all of the others who settled with him in the
New York colony named for the ship were Dutch
or German, he was called "Albert the Norman,"
and the small river with waterfall where he established his mill, in Albany, is still called Norman's
Kill. How could I doubt Power of Light after that
display of supernatural awareness?

During the half-decade since first making the
acquaintance of Björn, he has spoken frequently to
me of the peril to his work stemming from the
Dark Forces, or the forces of evil. Frankly, it
sounded rather paranoid to me. Since I am an
eternal optimist who has been taught that we should
try to see the good in everyone, Satan is not my
favorite topic of conversation. However, after becoming acquainted with Frederick and John I was
surprised to hear them constantly warning of the
Dark Forces that are at work throughout the earth,
and of the desperate need to warn those of good
will against "the evil ones who are doing Satan's
work among us."

Both men were insistent that a commentary on
this threatening force should be included in my
manuscript, and I (who have usually censored my
Guides' references to Satan) was equally insistent
that it had no place in a book about extraterrestrials.

"But it does!" Frederick exclaimed. "Your readers should be warned about how the Dark Side interferes in their human affairs and makes it especially difficult for the space people to help us.''

My Guides, when consulted, agreed with Frederick, saying: ''As for the Dark Forces, indeed they are having a field day in today's world, and making it extremely difficult for highly evolved space beings to work among you.'' I was also aware that Björn accuses these same Dark Forces, working through the oil cartels, of blocking international acceptance of his clean-energy invention that could (he says) obviate the necessity of burning fossil fuels, which pollute our atmosphere while also robbing Mother Earth of her riches.

I therefore asked Frederick to characterize the Dark Forces, and he replied: ''The Dark Side, or what people call evil, is the misapplication of the soul's free will when it goes against, or acts out of harmony with the immutable laws of the universe. God created no bad forces. Evil is only wrongly applied, or wrongly used, energy. This happens when souls become selfish and act for their own personal, selfish ends at the expense of the whole. All of these selfish acts create bad karma, which is a disturbance in the harmonious force of nature. Nature, when left alone, is the expression of harmonious vibration creating harmonious forms. That is beauty. If we observe life we see that there is a balance between all natural elements, including birds, trees and animals, and all such elements are unconsciously in tune with the Creator's plans. Man is the only expression on this planet created with free will, and he was meant to add to and not subtract from harmony.

''However, if man uses his free will to destroy, to abuse, and to exploit for selfish reasons he is out of harmony with the natural order. We reap what we sow, because whatever energy we put out will return to us in kind. If we break the immutable laws of nature, we create discord. Evil is the creation of man when he refuses to cooperate with nature's laws of balance. If we take and do not give back we create imbalance, which is a debt that must be settled. This imbalance registers in our thought-body, or astral body, and we carry it wherever we go. Because we carry this imbalance within ourselves we attract it wherever we are. This creates an imbalance in the natural flow of energy in nature, and life will deal us whatever blows are necessary to make us give back what we have taken. That is why selfishness and greed create evil and make us suffer. Nature exacts every debt.''

John then took up the thread of conversation, saying: ''Whenever we act selfishly, with unwarranted anger, greed, aggression and fear, we create disturbances in the psychic atmosphere of our planet and make it almost impossible for the space people to communicate with us, because our enegies shut them out. Thus there is an evil cloud of disruptive energy surrounding the earth and acting like static on a radio that makes it impossible to tune in to certain radio frequencies. That is also why it is so difficult for many Walk-ins, who come from a higher dimension, to stay on the track when they come here. These earth vibrations are so disruptive that they lose contact with the higher source, and many unfortunately lose their way, forgetting entirely the purpose for which they came back. This earth is really a danger zone. That is why total discipline, with adherence to the impersonal, impartial, immutable laws of nature is the only way out for any spiritual, seeking soul. We must be examples of the truth, shining and radiant, if we hope to succeed. Those who falter must make every effort to maintain that balance, or they too will fall under the influence of the Dark Side.

"We must realize that just as there are souls working tirelessly to restore balance and harmony to our wounded planet, so are there evil souls working for its destruction. These are souls that are consciously evil, and who enjoy the temporary power given to them by controlling the minds of ignorant people, inspiring in them thoughts of selfishness, fear, guilt and bigotry. It is these vibrations that our space friends are trying to eliminate from this planet. If the evil ones succeed, they will end up by destroying this planet and the life forms on it, with their discord. By creating harmony and cooperation with nature's laws, we reestablish balance and make conditions suitable for communication with the space people. That is our challenge!"

Frederick said that at the beginning of creation, all souls were fully conscious of being one with God. They realized that they were "just infinite expressions of the I AM, like the one sun that is reflected in a thousand buckets of water." Continuing, he declared, "Everything that exists in the material world is a thought vibration, however, and when the souls began to attach themselves to ideas, they created in their minds the idea of separateness. When we look without we see diversity and think that we are each separate, but when we look within to our own consciousness, we realize that everything is a manifestation of God, and thus we are not separate from anything. It is like the dandelion. All the spires of the dandelion shoot out toward the periphery, but they are all joined at the center. Satan is God turned backwards, because he wishes to possess and control everything in the outer world. God does not wish to possess and control because He *is* everything.''

After digesting this material, at least in part, I asked if the Guides could offer a more simplified definition, and they wrote: ''As to the Dark Forces, they stem from the buildup of all the evil that has occurred on earth since its beginning. Evil builds up just as the Group Mind that we wrote about in *Strangers Among Us* builds up with universal wisdom and good. The evil buildup becomes so tenacious that it is almost impossible to destroy without the cleansing of the planet that will occur at the time of the shift. That will give earthlings a new start and create a harmony that has not been known on earth since the early beginnings that the Bible calls the Days of Eden, before sin entered into man's consciousness, and selfishness and greed became rampant on the earth.''

Both Frederick and my Guides say that Satan was indeed a fallen angel, an actual being who set his will against God's, but that his power has grown as evil builds up on earth, just as the Christ Consciousness permeates the world and can build up goodness.

I asked the Guides for any final comments on the subject, and they obligingly wrote: ''As for the Dark Forces and Satan's role, why not point out that in Biblical lore Satan was the one who was exiled from heaven and came to earth to attempt a takeover. But when the New Age dawns at the close of this century the evil ones will be left there to perish, either then or shortly thereafter, when they will lack sustenance and friends. The Antichrist is now in flesh, as we have told you in previous books, and is still in school, but we do not wish to discuss him further at this time. We are keeping an eye on him, as are many others, and will alert those of good will when the time is right to clip his sails.''

I then asked if Björn Örtenheim would be successful in finding the right spot to float his platform in the bay off Maui, and they replied: "He should succeed, because it is part of the universal plan that this crystal and power center be made known in this era. Other discoveries that will prove the prior existence of Lemuria will also occur, and Björn is right in saying that Maui and some other parts of Lemuria will rise and survive the shift, although it will be perilous times there during the shift, as the tidal waves roar in. Better to take to the caves in the mountains if he wishes to remain there to witness that cosmic event.''

Afterword

> *. . . there is no new thing under
> the sun.*
> ECCLESIASTES 1:9

THAT familiar Biblical quotation succinctly sums up what the Guides and many experts are saying about UFOs and the earthly visitations of our space friends. They have been coming here from the beginning of time, but only when dire calamity seems threatened do they make their presence known in such overwhelming numbers as they are doing today.

The Old Testament account by the Prophet Ezekiel of his encounter with four space aliens, who took him in a UFO from Babylon to Jerusalem, is a case in point. In the sixth century B.C. the

Jewish race was in grave danger of extinction through absorption. King Nebuchadnezzar had besieged Jerusalem three times, taking captive 10,000 craftsmen, artisans, brave warriors and princes, including Ezekiel, and also carrying off to Babylon all of the treasures and golden vessels from King Solomon's Temple. Only the poorest of the poor were left in Palestine, and the absent Ezekiel worried about those leaderless Jews who were forsaking the one God and intermarrying with soldiers of the occupational army.

Ezekiel had been a captive in Babylon for more than thirty years when one day, while sitting by the river Chebar, he beheld a UFO approaching from the north and landing by his side. The Book of Ezekiel gives a graphic description of the flying saucer and of the four men who emerged from it, and tells of his trial run that day in the flying machine. Although nearly scared out of his wits, he bravely visited the spot a week later and again saw the UFO with its occupants. On his third encounter he actually flew with them to Jerusalem, where he visited the devastated city and the desecrated Temple for several days, talking to the Jews, before the spaceship returned and flew him back to Babylon.

There are many other such examples. Science writer Brad Lemley pointed out in the *Washington Post Magazine* that in the fifteenth century B.C. King Thutmose III of the Egyptian Eighteenth Dynasty saw "a circle of fire coming in the sky . . . one rod long was its body, and a rod wide, and it was noiseless," and the sky was later filled with many such circles (or flying saucers). In 329 B.C. two shining silver shields dived repeatedly at the army of Alexander the Great; and in Germany in

1561 "the sky was filled with cylindrical shapes from which emerged black, red, orange and blue-white spheres that darted about," a good description of a mothership releasing her cargo of flying saucers. And all of these occurrences, remember, were in the days when nothing was supposed to be flitting about in our skies except birds.

Numerous UFO sightings occurred in the late nineteenth and early twentieth century, but the rash of modern-day sightings dates from June 24, 1947, when Deputy U.S. Marshal Kenneth Arnold, piloting his private plane, spotted nine disks flying in formation "like a saucer would if you skipped it across the water," and the term "flying saucer" was born.

A number of people have written about an alleged encounter that President Dwight D. Eisenhower had with a small fleet of UFOs and their alien occupants at Edwards Air Force Base in California in 1954. Although no official report has ever been released, the Earl of Clancarty, a member of the British Parliament and author of several books on UFOs, recently revived the sensational story in the *National Enquirer* by declaring that he was personally told of the secret meeting by a former U.S. test pilot, who said that he was one of only six persons with Eisenhower at the time. Lord Clancarty, who heads a House of Lords group that is demanding British government declassification of UFO data, said that the test pilot told him: "Five different alien craft landed at the base. Three were saucer-shaped and two were cigar-shaped . . . the aliens looked something like humans, but not exactly."

According to this account, President Eisenhower was vacationing in nearby Palm Springs at the time, and was apparently summoned to the air force base by military officials. There, as he watched, the humanoids disembarked from their craft, talked to Ike in English, and displayed their spacecraft technology for him. The pilot said that they also demonstrated their ability to make themselves invisible and then to reappear, but that the president told them he did not think our world was ready to know of their presence, because it could cause "panic." The pilot claimed that they were all sworn to secrecy, but that he was now speaking out because all of the other witnesses to the encounter are dead.

In the mid-1950s a sergeant told Los Angeles UFO expert Gabe Green about that alleged landing at Edwards Air Force Base, saying, "I was at gunnery practice, under the command of a general. We were shooting live ammo at targets when all of a sudden five UFOs flew right over us. The general ordered all batteries to open fire on the craft. We did, but our shells had no effect whatsoever. We all stopped firing and watched the UFOs land at one of the large hangars."

I asked the Guides about the validity of these astonishing reports, and they replied: "Ike saw and spoke with the space aliens and should have released that fact before he died. He saw the spaceships as well."

Several of the extraterrestrials who contact me through the Guides have been promising that I would have a personal encounter while writing this book. The promise has yet to be fulfilled, and they explain that it is because I am too inaccessible to them, living as I do in a cooperative apartment building on one of the busiest thoroughfares in the nation's capital.

One of them wrote: "We need to find an area in which we are able to make contact without arousing too much attention. We want to show you our spaceship and controls, and talk about the purposes of our frequent visits to the earth plane, for we are here to study and to lead, if those willing to take an adventure in stride will cooperate, and not harm us. But that is why we have had to be so careful, for there are those who would dissect us, or keep us in captivity, when our systems are not geared to long stays in the earth's atmosphere. We come and go, replenishing our fuel supplies through a means not yet understood in your plane, and we need also to rejuvenate ourselves in the astroplane or we would surely die, as do earthlings, for we are not meant to live in that environment. Yet we do have permission from the Most High to make these voyages and to help earthlings catch up with our superior technological and spiritual developments. Be patient. We will find a way to contact you safely, and you will be unharmed."

Another day the Guides said that the space person was again with them to communicate some thoughts. "Ruth, this is Lordin from the Arcturus group," he began. "We come from a long way off, but are able to dissolve and reassemble atoms so that when we appear there we are in a form similar to that on our own planet as well as yours. When in the earth plane we are solid and flexible, and are not imaginary or hallucinatory. We are touchable and feelable, so that it is not necessary to be in an altered state of consciousness to see us, but some of us are more willing to establish contact than others. We are real, and it is urgent that earth people begin to realize the help that we are offering to prevent wars and prepare for evacuation operations before the shift. There will be flying machines to remove some of the earth people who are too valuable to be allowed to go into spirit, because of the need for their wisdom. We will take them to safety in the outer atmosphere, returning them after the shift if that is possible, and we believe that it will be. As for yourself, you will be working with us whether in spirit or in flesh, but it may be that we will want to lift you off rather than let you go into spirit."

Frankly, I'm not holding my breath until they "rescue" me. I'll admit that I'm never in lonely places by myself. I no longer drive a car, so I can't stage a rendezvous with a UFO in the remote countryside. But if the space aliens are so adept at materializing themselves, why can't they suddenly "appear" in my bedroom at night? Or is it vital for a spacecraft to be nearby? If so, I'll admit that there's no place to park one unseen in my busy locale.

The Guides say that "not since the beginning of recorded history has there been such an influx of space beings, due to the approaching shift and their desire to preserve records and botanical specimens. The sudden temperature alterations in all parts of the globe, when the shift occurs, will affect the trees and smaller growth, and they want these precious seedlings rescued so that they will be available for regrowth in acclimated areas, just as they want also to preserve advancements in science and medicine for the future generations. Given such a head start they will be able quickly to restore the quality of life that is good and eradicate that which is bad after the shift. They are already working through others in high places to preserve and rescue, and more is being done than can now be known."

My spirit pen pals insist that galactic fleets are continuing to orbit the earth, and will lift off a number of humans before the shift, but they add: "It is nonsense to expect them to take huge numbers of earthlings off in spaceships to other planets and galaxies. That is fiction. Earthlings are not able to survive in other atmospheres in their present bodies, but between lives large numbers of those who physically perish at the hour of the shift may work in other planetary systems in different forms, since there will be little opportunity for large masses to return to earth until the population again builds up to where sufficient numbers of bodies are available. In such a way we learn and progress." Apparently, then, those who are "lifted off" before the shift will remain on motherships until the earth settles into its new orbit, and a safe landing can be effected.

I asked how the extraterrestrials are working to help prevent World War III, which the Guides had previously warned could begin in 1986 in Ethiopia unless herculean efforts were made to prevent it. Their reply was this: "Space beings are trying to infiltrate into the war councils and strategy huddles of many nations to convince them of the folly of moves that would cause a world conflagration. Ethiopia is so stricken with famine, and so surprised by the good offices of Western nations [in sending food supplies], that the tension there will ease and may not now erupt into war with its neighbors, thus setting off the dread conflagration. It is not yet clear, but it looks now like war will not occur in 1986 or soon thereafter. If not, there will be a period of uneasy peace, with great technological advances, and extraterrestrials will play an active role in furthering some remarkable discoveries in that field.''

The Guides then gave an interesting blueprint of what they foresee for the next ten or fifteen years, if war is averted. Industry, they said, ''will blossom out into the most interlocking and coherent force in earth's history. Computers will require less space and fewer operators as centralization of data spreads to almost every segment of the economy. Those in charge of programming these central stations will have to be of the highest caliber, as false information and dangerous theories fed into the central data banks can permeate the thinking of all peoples and sway public opinion.

''There is real danger of a few evil people slipping into these positions in order to disrupt important work and governmental economies, or to control universal thought and action. Unless these central offices are guarded and patrolled, such activity can lead to war. Never before in world history has there been such potential for a few wrong-minded people to control the masses; yet never has there been so much potential for good if right-thinking, peace-loving people are there to direct the machines that will be 'read' daily by many millions in schools, offices and homes. Lives will be saved, time conserved, and a new life style emerge as people take their informational readouts from computers.

''Russia is devising an electronic system that will be able to knock out U.S. communications at the press of a button. Communication with orbiting satellites could then be lost, and the U.S. thereby shut off from quick information and powerless to respond if a surprise attack should be launched at that time. Books and newspapers will continue to attract thinking people, but others will take the easy way of learning through radio and television, until Russia demonstrates that the present culture is at the mercy of electronic gadgetry. Better to be developing some rival systems of power from the sun and wind, so that America is not left powerless in the event that Russia decides to negate the present sources of electrical energy.

"In the twenty-first century, after the shift, women will be equal with men and racial prejudice will be eradicated as a new race of people is reborn into the earth. When electrical power is restored after the shift, television and radio will largely assume the teaching role, instead of schools. Computers no larger than a human brain will make contact with intelligent beings in other planetary systems, and much will be learned from their superior technological and spiritual development."

The Guides say that after the shift of the earth on its axis scientific advancement will be in abeyance for a time "while people work on their soul and spiritual awareness. It will be an interesting time as these new souls from outer space blend with the earthlings to bring about an equilibrium between science and self-understanding."

I asked why there are so many indiscriminate killers on the earth today, and they replied: "The reason is that the Atlanteans of the latter destructive period are making their last-ditch fight, albeit subconsciously, to deface the beautiful earth and its peoples. They are wicked and have learned nothing through these long ages, when rebirths should have given them other interests and led them to review their past mistakes. They are a dying breed on earth and will be replaced by the gentle Lemurians, who will make less progress in scientific fields while making the earth a paradise of peaceable kingdoms. Those who have lived on other planets are also seeding the earth with a new breed that will accomplish much in establishing the kind of government and social ethos that will lead to peace. They fear that unless they volunteer for this project the earth will destroy itself and upset the orbiting alignment that for so long has stood the universe in good stead. They, like earthlings, are original sparks from the Godhead who have trained in other dimensions and times, and are willing to extend their knowledge beyond their own spheres.''

The Guides reiterate that although through free will humankind can prevent World War III, we cannot prevent the predicted shift at the end of this century. "Thoughts have a great deal to do with preventing war and other man-made disasters," they explain, "but there is no way to interfere with universal law, and earth is approaching that period when it is out of balance in the galaxy and will have to shift, a cleansing process that is needed to restore equations and deliver man from his own weaknesses and greed.''

In the early spring of 1984, as I was preparing to leave on a radio-television tour for the paperback edition of *Threshold to Tomorrow*, the publisher's publicity department asked if the Guides would be willing to make a prediction about the outcome of the Democratic primaries, which were then at fever pitch. On March 14 I therefore asked the Guides particularly about Gary Hart, who at the time seemed to be leading all other contenders, and they responded: "Hart will make a good showing but will not win the nomination. That will go to

Mondale, and Reagan will defeat him, but will be unable to serve out his second term. George Bush will therefore succeed him as president.''

In late October I again asked about the election outcome, and the Guides wrote: ''The election will be the predicted landslide for Reagan, but he will not serve out a second term. Bush will take over and be a good president, almost an outstanding one, for he will have the sympathy of the people and be firm in fulfilling the promises while not giving in to the extreme right or left. A good straight course. The deficit will continue to increase until that event of which we have just spoken occurs. Then taxes will be raised, and with the economy soaring, the deficit will be whittled down rapidly.''

I reminded them that they had earlier called Reagan a one-term president, and they responded, ''That is not far off base.'' They then told me what they claim will occur to place Bush in the highest office, and the approximate timing, but I do not wish to disclose it here for obvious reasons.

I also want to point out that the Guides are not always right in their political predictions. Their batting average is phenomenal, as when in 1971 they said that Ted Kennedy would never be elected U.S. president, nor would a woman in this century, although Great Britain would soon have a woman prime minister who was a Tory. In subsequent years they have been equally accurate about their forecasts concerning Jimmy Carter, Jerry Brown, Walter Mondale, China's Strongman Deng Xiaoping and his right turn toward capitalism, and numerous other leaders and nations.

But after correctly predicting the unexpected nomination and election of Jimmy Carter well before the event, and simultaneously declaring that he would be a one-term president, they flubbed their lines by saying that he would be succeeded by another Democrat who would be a big spender. I duly apologized for their error in my last previous book, but numerous readers wrote in to say that no apology was necessary, since Reagan had been a New Deal Democrat most of his adult life, and that he was certainly a big spender, if for defense rather than welfare.

Nevertheless, I think the Guides goofed on that one, and I hope that they're wrong again about Ronald Reagan this time. Better that he continues to thrive, for we need his buoyant optimism in these troubled times.

The Guides have reiterated their previous prediction that in the decade of the 1990s the American people will knowingly elect a Walk-in as president. They now say of him: "He will not emerge as a strong contender until 1992 or 1996, but he will become a world leader who will harness the energies of the people and guide them aright." They see no reason to alter their previous predictions about safe areas during and after the shift, and they add that if World War III is averted, Africa will be a "relatively secure area" for increased settlement.

I asked for any final comments about our friends from outer space, and they wrote: "They will continue to arrive in increasing numbers as Walk-ins, and will be of inestimable value in leading people to safe areas; also in preparing them for the hardships during and for a time after the shift. The extraterrestrials—the ones who materialize there by reassembling the atoms—are active as well, and will direct rescue operations and sound warnings in various ways to alert those who wish to move to safer areas and establish settlements there. As we have said before, many of them will remain for some time after the shift to help establish the New Age and teach earthlings what they have learned on their more enlightened planets: that although a body is a handy implement for getting around and performing one's appointed tasks, the spirit or soul is the real *you,* and it was for that that the universe was created.

"Thus, it is far better to lose one's body and preserve one's soul on a higher plateau than to save one's skin, so to speak, by crowding others out of the way and thinking solely of one's own rescue. We are our soul! We are not our body! That is simply a costume that we are permitted to wear for a brief moment in time; but we, like time, are forever!"

So welcome, space friends. We're happy to have you aboard!

Appendix

READERS who wish to contact any of the following people discussed in this book may write to them at the addresses given below. Please remember to enclose a stamped, self-addressed envelope if you are requesting a reply from them or from me. But please do not ask me to query the Guides for or about you. Because of so many thousands of requests, they can no longer comply.

John Andreadis
PO Box 6046 FDR Station
New York, NY 10150

William Goodlett
109 Union St.
Salem, VA 24153

Robert Hurlburt
PO Box 264
North Hampton, NH 03862

Dr. J. Allen Hynek and CUFOS
PO Box 1402
Evanston, IL 60204

Charlotte King
1100 Home Ave. #567
Sacramento, CA 95825

Ruth Montgomery
G. P. Putnam's Sons
200 Madison Ave.
New York, NY 10016

Joseph & Carol Ostrom
132 S. College Ave. #211
Ft. Collins, CO 80524

Björn Örtenheim
PO Box 1078
Makawao, Maui, HI 96768

and

Stenhuggarens väg 13
Skokloster
S-19800 Bålsta,
Sweden

Peggy Otis
11293 W. Dorado
Littleton, CO 80127

David Paladin
Box 11942
Albuquerque, NM 87192

Dr. R. Leo Sprinkle
University of Wyoming
Box 3708 University Station
Laramie, WY 82071

Shirlee Teabo
226 S. 312th St.
Federal Way, WA 98003

Diane Tessman
PO Box 622
Poway, CA 92064

Tuella
PO Box 2566
Durango, CO 81301

Joyce & Hal Updike
Box 243
Ovid, CO 80744

Frederick Von Mierers & friends
PO Box 6046 FDR Station
New York, NY 10150

About the Author

Ruth Montgomery is one of America's most beloved writers. After many years as a syndicated Washington columnist on politics and world affairs, she turned her attention to spiritual and psychic matters. She has written one best-seller after another, including A WORLD BEYOND, the after-death revelations of medium Arthur Ford; HERE AND HEREAFTER, a visionary work on reincarnation; and STRANGERS AMONG US, in which she first told the world of the Walk-ins, who are further described in her most recent book, THRESHOLD TO TOMORROW. With ALIENS AMONG US, Mrs. Montgomery continues her work of informing and enlightening mankind.

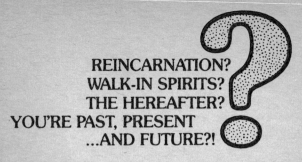

REINCARNATION?
WALK-IN SPIRITS?
THE HEREAFTER?
YOU'RE PAST, PRESENT
...AND FUTURE?!

OBSERVE THE OCCULT...
FAWCETT NON-FICTION
by
Ruth Montgomery